Twilight, True Love and You

SEVEN SECRETS TO FINDING YOUR EDWARD OR JACOB

LOUISE DEACON

summersdale

TWILIGHT, TRUE LOVE AND YOU

Summersdale Publishers Ltd
46 West Street
Chichester
West Sussex
PO19 1RP
UK

www.summersdale.com

Printed and bound in Great Britain

ISBN: 978-1-84953-140-5

Substantial discounts on bulk quantities of Summersdale books are available to corporations, professional associations and other organisations. For details contact Summersdale Publishers by telephone: +44 (0) 1243 771107, fax: +44 (0) 1243 786300 or email: nicky@summersdale.com.

Personality scales used within the book have been adapted from IPIP

This book is not associated with or authorised by Stephenie Meyer or her publishers

CONTENTS

Photography by Nicky Jane

Note From the Author

I am a chartered clinical psychologist with 21 years' experience of helping people with their personal difficulties. I specialise in the area of relationships and sexual health, and many of my clients are young people facing problems in their love lives. An important focus of my work is helping them make better relationship choices in the future. Although this book is based on the understandings I have gained, because of confidentiality I have not used any client material. The case examples in this book are based on people I have spoken to in my personal life who were happy to share their story.

I first became aware of the significance of *Twilight* when I went to see the films at the cinema. I was stunned by the way the girls in the audience reacted. They sighed, gasped and screamed. Never before had I witnessed such a strong emotional reaction in public to a film. As a psychologist I was fascinated.

I had already been struck by the power of romantic fiction in influencing people's relationship decisions. I had heard many a young woman say she had stayed in an unhappy relationship because she had assumed her love story would play out as it does in books and films, that her boyfriend would change and there would be a happy ending.

When I read the *Twilight* saga, I realised why it had captivated millions. The saga is perfectly crafted to appeal to the psychology of today's woman. Not only has it captured our imagination and emotions, but the *Twilight* story has the potential to shape your life. The story can have a powerful impact on your views of men and love.

So I wrote this book to help you uncover what *Twilight* means for you and your life, and to help you navigate your way around the pitfalls of today's relationships to find true love.

ABOUT THIS BOOK

This book will deepen your understanding of *Twilight*, reveal the relevance of the saga to your own personal life and show you how to find a man who can be your true love. Some girls are lucky in love and have an instinctive ability to recognise the man who can make them happy. They can't explain how they do it. Their success is a secret, even to themselves. But in this book the mystery is revealed for *Twilight* fans.

THE *TWILIGHT* SECRETS

Secret One: The Power of Twilight *Revealed*
Discover why Edward and Jacob appeal to your deepest human needs.

Secret Two: Discover the Hidden Dangers of Your Romantic Imagination
Understand how *Twilight* has shaped the way you look at men.

Secret Three: Loving a Human
Examine the truth about your feelings for Edward and Jacob, and find out why only a human can fulfil your needs as a woman.

Secret Four: Knowing Yourself
Explore Bella's character and needs in a relationship, and discover how to learn more about your own character and needs.

Secret Five: How to Get a Deep Insight Into Your Boyfriend
Examine how Bella saw Edward and how you can uncover the truth about your boyfriend's personality.

Secret Six: How to Know if Your Relationship Really Works
Learn how Edward and Bella worked as a couple and the ways you can develop insight into how your relationship works.

Secret Seven: How to Predict Your Future With Your Boyfriend
Discover how to predict your future together.

The Power of *Twilight* Revealed

(It's not just because they're great books!)

CHAPTER 1

WILL YOU FIND YOUR EDWARD? WILL YOU FIND YOUR JACOB?

Bella Swan arrived in Forks, alone and miserable.

She'd left her home in sunny Phoenix, the city she loved, to live in the rainy Olympic Peninsula with Charlie, the father she'd barely seen for three years. She'd never fitted in and was dreading facing a new high school.

On her first day, she was placed next to the stunningly handsome Edward Cullen in biology class. Before long, she was deeply in love and her life was transformed.

Could this be you? Or is it just a fantasy story? Can our lives be transformed by finding a perfect love?

YOUR DILEMMA

Is your boyfriend or next boyfriend going to be 'Your Edward'? Is he 'Your Jacob'?

This is the question millions of you all over the world are asking after reading Stephenie Meyer's *Twilight* series. The story is so powerful that it has changed the way you look at your own love life. In some ways, this could be a good thing. You're no longer willing to settle for someone who doesn't love you enough.

But there are dangers, too. The romantic ideas portrayed in *Twilight* may lead you to a boyfriend who cannot make you happy and might even be dangerous.

And there's another problem when you love *Twilight*. The man of your dreams is not a human being. He is immortal, has superhuman powers and diamond skin (if you are Team Edward), or can change his shape at will (if you are Team Jacob). He loves you with a tender, fierce, eternal devotion. He'd rather die than live without you. He'd surrender his life to protect you. The dilemma for you is: after Edward's topaz-eyed, chiselled perfection and Jacob's six-pack, how can any normal human mortal measure up?

LOVE IS HARD TO FIND

It was already difficult enough to find someone who is right for you. In fact, it's harder now than it's ever been. You've more freedom and choice about who your boyfriend is than at any other time in history. Now that travel is fast and relatively cheap you have the opportunity to meet hundreds of guys in your normal, day-to-day life. On a computer you can connect to someone anywhere in the world in a second.

Take Bella. On her first day at Forks High School she met Eric and Mike, both nice enough local boys, and she could immediately sense that both were interested in her. The school cafeteria held plenty more boyfriend possibilities.

The choice of potential boyfriends is breathtaking nowadays (even if many of these guys are not breathtaking themselves!). So what's the problem? Psychology studies of decision-making reveal that the more options you have, the more difficult it is to make your choice. In medieval times there was no cafeteria full of guys – it might have been a choice between Godfrey the farmer from up the hill (dark-skinned, well-built, makes you laugh but has teeth missing) or Cuthbert the farmer from down the hill (red hair, good teeth, but keeps on repeating that boring joke about the virgin and the bishop).

Back then you didn't have much to ponder over. It was likely your father would be the one making the decision over who you should marry. Even if you were lucky and he took your feelings into account, you didn't have much time to decide. If you dithered for too long, you'd be an old maid. If you were 18 and unmarried, everyone would be whispering about you behind your back. Your mother would be mortified and trying to get you into a convent. Anyway, the choice between Godfrey or Cuthbert didn't matter all that much. If you got married, there was a good chance that one of you would be dead in a few years (childbirth, plague, starvation) so you probably wouldn't have been committing yourself to years and years with him.

Nowadays you have numerous options and plenty of time to make your choice, and it's a big decision. With today's longer life expectancies, you have a good chance of spending 50 years plus with your partner. But that is not the only thing making your choice harder. In modern life you often have very little information to go on about a guy apart from what he tells you. In the old days, you may have known him from childhood or at least would be aware of his reputation from your network of family and friends. People have always loved gossip, and in a small village with no TV or books you would be privy to practically everything there is to know about your neighbours. You would know that dark-haired, muscle-bound Godfrey had a terrible temper and red-headed Cuthbert was unreliable.

But today you could have an experience like Lauren's:

Lauren, a 19-year-old trainee veterinary nurse, signed up to an Internet dating agency. 'I split up with the boyfriend I'd been seeing since I was at school. For months afterwards, I never seemed to meet anyone who captured my imagination. Every weekend I ended up socialising with the same people. They were a good crowd of friends whom I'd known for years but I wasn't meeting anyone new. So I decided to try my luck at Internet dating.'

Lauren soon met Mark, who sounded perfect on his profile. He said he was 25, earned over £30,000 a year, and was looking for the right girl. 'We met up. It was a fabulous evening. He gazed into my eyes and told me I was "the one". We went on a few more dates, and after only a few weeks I fell hopelessly in love.'

What he didn't tell her was that he was addicted to gambling on fruit machines. He was not interested in the slightest in having a long-term relationship. He was really looking for no-strings fun.

'I found all this out gradually over several months. He's not the person he seemed to be at the start.'

Because she didn't know anyone who knew him, she was completely in the dark. If she'd talked to any of his friends – both male and female – she'd have found out that Mark had a reputation for gambling and cheating on his girlfriends. But all she had to go on were the dating site profile Mark had written himself and her own judgements.

And you may well be in the same position. It's tough, very tough, to judge other people accurately – especially when it's a man who's doing his best to impress you. If you fall in love with him, it's often too late. 'Imprinting' is not just something that happens to shape-shifters. Once you have 'imprinted' on someone, it is not easy to change your feelings, even if you uncover all sorts of unpleasant things about them.

Lauren is still seeing Mark. 'I know he has a wandering eye at times and doesn't always tell the truth… but I still love him.'

How many times have you heard your female friends saying similar things: 'I know he is bad for me/is selfish/treats me badly/ has been unfaithful/hits me... but I still love him!'

YOU NEED LOVE MORE THAN EVER

There is nothing wrong with wanting to be loved. As a human being, you've always needed love. Almost all people crave companionship with others. Our survival depends on the attachments we form with each other. Your longing for love – just like Bella's – is completely natural.

But in modern life we're told we must function as an individual. We're given the message that a modern young woman should be independent and happy on her own. It's very common for families to be scattered and broken, like Bella's. We often don't know most of the people who live around us. It's considered normal to leave home for college, university or a job, or to live on our own, or move across the country to a new town. But today's independent lifestyles don't fully satisfy a basic human need: the need to feel special to other people. So we long for a boyfriend who can share our day-to-day life, a man who'll be interested in the intimate details of our lives, a boyfriend who'll care if we are happy or sad, bored or lonely.

And it gets worse, because these longings inside us get stronger every single day. Every time we turn on the radio, switch on the TV, pick up a magazine or listen to music, we are bombarded with love stories. Love songs and stories that pull on our emotions and shape our thoughts. With an MP3 player in our pocket and a paperback crammed into our handbag, we are carrying the same repeated message: love is a wonderful, powerful force, and we need it now!

Being exposed to all this idealised, romantic material naturally makes us want love more. The pressures of modern life make us hungry for love and the diet of romance in the media makes us ravenous. It's as if we have been kept half starved and made to spend our spare time reading recipe books over and over again.

And then *Twilight* came along.

TWILIGHT HAS TAKEN THE LOVE STORY TO ANOTHER LEVEL

It's not just another story about an ordinary man who loves a woman. Stephenie Meyer has described how the *Twilight* story came to her in a dream. The characters came from deep within her subconscious, where her basic longings are buried. It's likely that you share those longings and *Twilight* has spoken to your deepest needs, for a man who will love you unconditionally and eternally, and you are ready to take the fantasy man to another extreme. Edward and Jacob are more like gods than human beings – they are immortal, give eternal love, have immense powers and are wise and fierce protectors.

Although you may believe in God, it's quite likely that God doesn't play a big part in your daily emotional life. The younger you are, the less likely you are to be involved with the Church. In the UK it is estimated that only around 6 per cent of 20- to 29-year-olds and 3 per cent of 15- to 19-year-olds go to church regularly. And these figures are going down year by year. This leaves a gap because if you don't have a deeply held faith, you no longer have the sense of security which comes from feeling loved and protected by a mighty creator. This is where Edward and Jacob come in. For many young women, the *Twilight* heroes touch a powerful set of feelings: their need for love, romance and God.

There is nothing wrong with this in itself. But *Twilight* is such a powerful story it not only affects the way that young women look at men but also may influence the way they make relationship decisions. Girls all over the world are ending relationships because 'He's not my Edward/Jacob'.

 Monica is 20 and at university studying sports science. She had been seeing Raj, a medical student, but soon after reading Twilight *she ended the relationship because Raj was not offering anything like the unconditional love that Bella had from Edward. Now when she meets a man she thinks, 'Is he my Edward?' She is still single and has decided none of her fellow students could ever measure up to her ideal.*

Others are looking for men who are exciting like Edward and Jacob; they would like their relationships to measure up to the drama of Bella's love life. The perils of being in love with a vampire or werewolf make a thrilling story. But these types of thrills don't translate very well to real life:

Kate is 16 and is fed up with dull, safe boys. She got bored in her last relationship as her boyfriend never wanted to do anything.

'He seemed happy just to come round to my house and stay in every night watching TV,' she said. 'His only conversation was about things that happened in class, or his last set of exam results.'

She split up from him and met Nick, an acquaintance of her older brother.

Nick couldn't have been more different. Nick had an energy about him that she couldn't resist. She sensed he had a rage bubbling beneath the surface, however: 'I saw him as a tiger on a leash.' She felt a thrill when she was with him, just like Bella when she first met Edward.

Then one day at a football match Nick battered a stranger unconscious over a joke about his favourite team.

Even if you are not the type of person to be drawn to dangerous boyfriends, there are other types of men who are unlikely to make any girl happy. The messages *Twilight* gives you about love could influence your choices, and make you more likely to fall for such a person. *Twilight* delivers the message that a miserable, tormented guy can be made whole by the power of love. Edward was an unhappy, tortured soul who spent all of his life unfulfilled until he met Bella. Through the transforming power of love, he eventually changed into a loving, happy husband, content just to be with Bella and their child.

This is a satisfying story, but it is not based on psychological truths. An unhappy, discontented young man makes an unhappy, discontented boyfriend. Love is a wonderful thing, but it does not change people's basic characters. *Twilight* makes men with complex, difficult personalities seem fascinating. These men make interesting cases for experienced therapists but they do not make good boyfriends:

Zena, a 21-year-old assistant manager of a well-known clothing store, was drawn to Joshua because he was 'deep'. He was handsome and had a brooding quality she found intriguing – he reminded her of Edward. 'He looked beneath the surface of everything. His way of being was a real contrast to the people at my day job. They only care about fashion and the latest eyelash extension technology. Joshua was a thinker.'

She loved to make him laugh, which he did rarely. As their relationship progressed, Zena tried to make him happy. She poured more and more energy into drawing him out. 'But he was unhappy. Unhappy with his job and his life. He hardly ever took pleasure in the things that I arranged for him. He'd shut himself in his room and turn his phone off for days.'

When she complained to him, he said he knew she'd turn on him in the end and that people always let him down. Exhausted, she eventually ended the relationship. She found out later he had made a (thankfully unsuccessful) suicide attempt.

THE SECRET OF HAPPY RELATIONSHIPS

The secret is not good communication or being prepared to work at the relationship. These are good things, and can certainly help, but there's something far more important.

It is to choose the right guy in the first place: a boyfriend who is capable of and interested in fulfilling your needs. This may sound obvious, but a huge number of us don't do it. The problem is it's all too easy to fall in love with someone who's incapable of making you happy.

THE DANGER OF 'IMPRINTING'

In *Breaking Dawn*, Jacob cannot help himself 'imprinting' on Renesmee, Bella's daughter. Imprinting is something to which the shape-shifters are vulnerable. They can form an immediate and unbreakable bond with another person. They have absolutely no choice and no control over their feelings.

As humans we go through something similar when we fall in love. We can't control who we fall in love with and although our love is not unbreakable we certainly can't fall out of love easily. We can't change our feelings just because we want to. When we truly fall for someone we become attached to them for a long time.

HOW WOMEN LOVE

When women fall in love, their feelings may be so strong that they'll be willing to put up with almost anything from their boyfriend. This is the way many women love. From my observations of couples I believe that, on the whole, girls are more likely than men to continue loving their partner, even if they don't fulfil their needs. Bella was willing to sacrifice her life for Edward – every time she was with him she risked death. This does not surprise us as readers because we know girls will do this.

Generally, as a female, you will be more likely than a man to love someone even if you're treated badly.

If you are lucky, you'll have a relationship in which you can fulfil each other's needs. If this happens, then your love will be enduring and you will be happy together.

But a lot of the time this doesn't happen.

The chances are that you will break up with a number of men before you get married or live with someone. And if you get married, statistics suggest that in the UK there is a 45 per cent chance of getting divorced.

Why does this happen? It's because it is all too easy for couples to fall in love even though they are unable to make each other happy in the long term.

WHY DO WE FALL IN LOVE WITH MEN WHO CANNOT MAKE US HAPPY?

At first, I thought all the girls I worked with were unlucky. They just happened to fall in love with men who later turned out to be wrong for them. I thought it couldn't be predicted – just one of life's quirks. Then I began thinking that there must be something in the women's childhoods that led them to be attracted to men who weren't right for them.

But this did not add up. Many of them had perfectly happy childhoods. And when I began uncovering the story of the unhappy relationship, it became obvious to me, as an outsider, that it was doomed almost from the beginning. There were signs from the start that the couple were incompatible. But the girl hadn't seen them.

What the girls had in common was that they had highly romantic ideas about the power of love to change their boyfriends so that eventually they would become the men they wanted. The women talked as if they were in the centre of a love story, where one day all the obstacles to their happiness would be overcome. Their ideas about love seemed to come from books or films rather than reality. From my work with couples and singles I realised that many women fall in love with very little insight into themselves and what they need from a relationship, and even less insight into their boyfriends. So it's no wonder that their relationships did not last.

The problem is that the romantic ideals that come from stories like *Twilight* can make love not only blind, but deaf and dumb as well. Many women fall in love blind to their own needs, blind to who their partner is and what he can give, and deaf to the warning bells – and this results in them making dumb mistakes. It is only after painful experience that women realise the truth.

Karima is a 23-year-old day-care nursery worker.

'I started dating Andy, a fireman, and I fell in love with him as soon as I saw him in his uniform. My heart did a somersault and I was gone. I was obsessed with him for the next three years.'

Those three years were full of constant arguments about money.

Andy lived for adventure and spent money without

worrying. He blew most of his salary on his expensive car. When Karima met him he was sleeping on a friend's sofa because he hated to 'waste' money on boring things like rent.

Karima was completely different. 'I'm careful with money and believe in investing in property. My dream is to buy a home of my own one day.' She persuaded him to save up for a deposit with her so that they could get a place together.

Then one day Andy came to her with the news that he'd spent his part of the deposit on a sports car that a friend was selling at a bargain price.

Karima felt betrayed and ended the relationship.

Was Karima right to feel betrayed? All of her friends were full of sympathy. Andy was just a selfish guy who wouldn't grow up. He had let her down, big time. But...

You could argue Andy was just being himself. He'd always preferred to live for the moment and spend his money on cars. He'd told her that, upfront. But because Karima needed a man who would be 'responsible' about money, she set about transforming Andy into the man she wanted. And she was disappointed because her attempts failed. She thought that if he loved her enough, he could change his basic nature. You could also argue she didn't really love the man he was. After all, she fell for him when she saw him in his fireman's outfit. Did she fall in love with the man – or the uniform?

After this difficult time in her life, Karima realised she needed a boyfriend who possessed a similar attitude about money to her own – a man who shared her dream of investing time and money in a flat. She gained insight into herself and what she needed from a man through painful experience.

DO YOU NEED TO GO THROUGH PAINFUL EXPERIENCES TO LEARN?

No, you don't. You don't need to experience putting your hand into the fire to know it will hurt. You don't need to jump off a cliff to learn that you'll break your neck at the bottom. You can learn all sorts of lessons without going through pain. You are an intelligent human being. You can make all sorts of discoveries with the power of your mind alone. You possess incredible powers of insight and perception, powers that set you above other species. So why not use them?

Stephenie Meyer's writing shows she has a profound understanding of the workings of the human heart. This is the secret of the *Twilight* series: the books reveal much about the psychology of young women.

Read on if you want to discover the messages and insights hidden in *Twilight*.

CHAPTER 2

WHY EDWARD AND JACOB HAVE CAPTURED YOUR HEART

YOUR DEEPEST HUMAN NEEDS

Twilight came to Stephenie Meyer in a dream.

The story sprang from her deepest, unconscious longings and *Twilight* speaks to your deepest needs, too.

As a sophisticated twenty-first-century woman, you can harness the latest technology to further your desires: mobile phones, computers and the Internet. You have highly developed powers of thought. You have been schooled for years and understand the world around you. You are rational, you can plan. You can make amazingly astute judgements at work and in your studies. You have incredible powers of discrimination and can process huge amounts of information. You are truly a being of higher intelligence.

And then all of that goes out the window when you meet a man. When it comes to men, the side of your brain that kicks in is primitive, emotional and hungry. It is the part of your brain that helped women survive hundreds of thousands of years ago.

Although you are modern and sophisticated, when it comes to emotions, your brain has not evolved since ancient times. Your instincts about men are the same as a cavewoman's.

You have the same emotional needs. Edward and Jacob have been crafted by Stephenie Meyer to appeal to those basic desires.

IS THERE SUCH A THING AS TRUE LOVE?

Yes! Love is an eternal emotion. Human beings have always loved each other. It is a basic part of our nature. Poems and stories from thousands of years ago speak of love.

Love is real – people all over the world experience the heart-pounding, overwhelming longing to be with that special person.

For many, the early exciting stage of new love settles down into a deeper, calmer state. But scientists have found that for some, the first flush of new love can last for years. A lucky 10 per cent of couples in long-term relationships remain in love in this way for decades. Psychologists call these couples 'swans', because swans mate for life. Stephenie Meyer may have decided to give Bella the surname Swan for this reason.

THE *TWILIGHT* HEROES ARE IRRESISTIBLE IN SEVEN WAYS

1) Edward and Jacob offer unconditional love

Your need for love is in your nature. Because we humans love each other, we look after each other. Because we look after each other, we survive.

You were born with an innate need for love, because without it you'd have died in infancy. Unless your parents or caregiver loved you enough to feed you and keep you safe and warm, you wouldn't have lived.

But your need for love is far more than just a way of getting your basic physical needs met. As a child, you can't develop properly without love. At its most extreme, children who are totally starved of love can develop what doctors call 'failure to thrive', where they become dull-eyed, listless and stop growing. In less extreme cases, if a child doesn't get enough love they'll grow up physically OK but will have problems with managing their emotions and behaviour.

When you have a parent or caregiver who responds to your emotional needs, your brain develops properly and you learn how to manage your feelings. You grow up with a security about yourself that makes it easier for you to handle relationships.

When you become an adult this need for love doesn't really go away. But never again will you find someone who will provide the same amount of unconditional, self-sacrificing love as a parent. In adult life, nobody else is going to make you the centre of their life the way that your mother probably did. Nobody else is going to spend hours just looking at you and delighting in every little move of yours, your stumbling awkwardness, your foibles, your weaknesses as well as your triumphs.

But Edward does!

He spends hours watching Bella sleep. He sees she is special and loves her despite her awkwardness and feebleness. She is the only focus in his life. He would die for her. He loves her with the intensity and obsession that in reality is only felt by a mother for her newborn baby.

Edward's feelings for Bella are unconditional. You can't help but respond to Edward emotionally because there is a part of you that still craves unconditional love from a powerful protector. When you grow up you realise your parents are not all-powerful and you see they are only human beings, with many faults and weaknesses of their own.

The unconditional love that Edward and Jacob offer is incredibly attractive. Imagine having someone fall in love with the person you are inside. The reality is that men are deeply swayed by your physical appearance. You probably put a lot of thought into the way you look. You are likely to spend a lot of effort on clothes, hair and make-up. Bella does nothing. She hates dressing up and wears baggy old clothes. She does nothing about maintaining her figure. She eats what she wants. She cooks big meals for herself and Charlie, and just grabs a granola bar whenever she feels like it.

We wish! We would love to have a man fall deeply in love with us however we looked, however we behaved.

We miss this unconditional love that only comes from our parents. Sadly, as an adult, the love you will receive from a man won't be like that. There will be all sorts of conditions on the love your man will have for you. Men and women fall out of love with each other all the time. You won't necessarily know what the conditions on his love are, and nor will he.

In a real relationship you'll have to give not just love, but time, attention and care. You'll have to accommodate his needs. Your role as his girlfriend comes with a whole range of duties and expectations, many of them unreasonable, time-consuming or just plain annoying, from listening to his attempts to play the guitar, to rescheduling your holiday in Spain with the girls to join him and his family at their static caravan in Cleethorpes. All Edward and Jacob want... is for Bella to be with them. Her love is enough. We feel that this is as it should be.

2) The way they look

You don't want to be loved by just anyone. You're naturally more attracted to good-looking men. Edward and Jacob are chiselled, hard, masculine and handsome. You're biologically wired to respond to looks like these. Handsome men with strong jaws, square faces, narrow hips and broad shoulders are likely to be healthy, vital and have plenty of testosterone. Poor 'baby-faced' Mike Newton doesn't stand a chance! Soft, rounded faces are not attractive to women, as they signal weakness and submissiveness. We like our babies to be cute and baby-faced – not our guys.

Anyone who's seen the *Twilight* films can't help but notice the gasps and sighs in the audience whenever Edward or Jacob take their tops off. The lean, muscular, very masculine bodies trigger a strong response in us. We may not be as obsessed with looks as men, but we can't help being drawn to the attributes of a fit, young hunter. And it helps that Edward has topaz eyes and diamond skin – a man who can fulfil your natural feminine desires for good looks and jewellery. Perfect!

Good looks alone are not enough, however: money, power and status are also important to women. Studies show most women would prefer to date an average-looking doctor than a handsome McDonald's worker.

But times are changing. Nowadays women take care of themselves financially and are demanding more from their guys. Young men are feeling the pressure to take greater care of their looks. *Twilight* is part of that pressure: it has changed things for men as well as women.

I interviewed a male fan of *Twilight*. Harry is 18 and is taking a year off before university. He is in a steady relationship. What struck me was he never talked about the love aspect of the *Twilight* books, but instead obsessed about the physical attributes of the heroes. His ideal is to look like Jacob. He goes to the gym most days and watches what he eats, avoiding fat and sticking to lean cuts of meat. His friends are similar – they argue about whose abs look most like Taylor Lautner's. Harry told me, without embarrassment, that he spends a lot of time posing in front of the mirror.

You'll still meet plenty of men who feel it's their right to tuck into as much beer and as many burgers as they like, take no exercise and yet think nothing of asking a gorgeous girl out. They expect their girl to be toned and groomed, but see no problem that they themselves have a belly hanging over their belt and clothes that look like they have been fished out of a skip.

But many men have grasped the fact that the dynamics between the sexes have changed. These men have discovered that women have eyes, too! They've listened to female friends talking about 'fit men' and feel the pressure to look good.

3) They are the ultimate hunters

It's 50,000 BC.

In *Cavewoman's Weekly* – between the articles on the latest fur-skin fashions and mud-based beauty products – there is an interview with a typical tribeswoman, Aggi, on what she looks for in an ideal mate.

Aggi says she dreams of an incredible hunter with amazing speed and strength. A man who'd provide any food she wanted in the stewing pot each night. A man who would feed her and her children meat so that they'd grow healthy and strong. A man who'd allow her to sleep peacefully at night; knowing any mountain lion that dared lay a paw in their cave would live to regret it. A man who'd save her life if an out-of-control mammoth came sliding towards her on the glacier.

Aggi would be describing Edward and Jacob.

These old instincts survive in us today. Although nowadays you're not likely to see your guy hunt for anything except the TV remote control, you still want a strong man who can take care of you and protect you. The cavewoman in you lives on and Edward and Jacob are the men of your dreams – mates with incredible physical prowess.

Read the following and compare how you feel about the two different guys:

Sean is lean and muscular because he needs to be physically fit for his job. You go for a weekend away with him and he swings your heavy bags (you felt it necessary to pack every single pair of shoes you own) over his shoulder without a second thought. He walks with a fast stride and can pick you up as effortlessly as if you were a size-zero supermodel.

Paul is out of condition and round-shouldered because his job involves sitting on an office chair all day. You go for a weekend away with him and he takes your heavy bags from you. He can barely lift them and after a few yards of puffing he plonks them on the floor with a groan. He says, 'Here, you carry them, I can't manage it. I was never very strong, even as a child.' He has to have a little sit down before you can move on.

Who do you find more attractive, Sean or Paul? It's likely that you prefer the stronger one. Imagine them going out to hunt. Sean would be striding back with a deer slung across his shoulders and Paul would be limping home, nursing bites on his legs after losing a battle with a rabbit.

We prefer physically powerful guys. We can't help it. Like Bella, we prefer the super-strong Edward and Jacob to Mike 'marshmallow' Newton. But in the modern world, a man who does physical work for a living almost certainly earns less than an office worker. Sean, a removals man, would be unable to provide as much as Paul, a tax accountant. These days, wielding a hefty bank balance matters more than wielding large muscles; yet we still get dragged back to our instinctive desire for biceps and abs.

4) They are warrior heroes

Edward and Jacob are the perfect fighting machines. They fight to protect Bella. They are willing to wage war with anyone who threatens her – including each other. They would lay down their lives for her.

This is music to the female soul. Aggi the cavewoman would have known that the biggest threat to her was not a marauding mountain lion. The biggest threat was other human beings. A man who was willing to fight for her was a fantastic mate for Aggi in ancient times.

And it's still pertinent today. Although equality has permeated many aspects of life and you can now do as you wish, your primitive instinct to find a warrior is alive and well.

Much of the *Twilight* series focuses on Edward and Jacob's desperate fight to protect Bella from the vampires who want to kill her. In today's bland life, most of us abide by civilised rules, and fighting is a crime. But the ancient scenario of warrior heroes fighting for their woman speaks to something deep within us.

5) Edward and Jacob do wonders for a woman's self-esteem

A healthy self-esteem is an important survival tool. If you believe you're special and important, you'll fight for your survival. You'll do the best for yourself and get the best treatment you can from others. As a result you will thrive.

When you stop thinking you are special and worthwhile, you get depressed. Bella is clearly showing signs of depression in the opening chapters of *Twilight*. She cries on her own, she avoids people, she neglects herself and she is full of negative thoughts. This all changes, however, by the end of the story, because of her relationship with Edward. He convinces her she is important. He restores her self-esteem.

Even though Bella doesn't have any special attributes and is not particularly beautiful, graceful, intelligent or successful, Edward and Jacob can see through this to her underlying lovability and specialness.

Your self-esteem is very sensitive to how other people view you. If the people around you value you and think you're important, you are more likely to believe it, too. Edward and Jacob bombard Bella with evidence of how important she is to them – as do the rest of the Cullens, Edward's vampire family.

Sadly, these days we don't get showered with adoration and appreciation from others. It's quite the opposite. Modern life is bruising for the self-esteem. You are not an important member of the tribe any more; you are a speck amongst six billion people. Most people on the planet do not have a clue who you are. Because we are shifting around and society is complicated, you are constantly having to go into new groups of people and work for acceptance. Approval and admiration is hard to find.

We want to believe we are special and unique and important to others, yet reality often jars with this. In life we get rejected, fail, are treated unfairly and don't get what we deserve. People say nasty things about us behind our backs, or even worse, are completely indifferent to us. You might be at the top of the tree in your studies or at work, but on a night out you could feel like the plainest, most awkward girl in the room – or the other way around.

Every emotionally healthy person believes that they are special. We are all convinced of our own uniqueness and seek someone who can confirm this for us. Time and again, psychology studies show we all believe we are better than the average person. Most of us believe we are better looking, cleverer, more organised, fairer minded and more interesting than the average person. Ideally, we would like others to recognise this, too.

Finding a boyfriend is a good boost to one's self-esteem. But the *Twilight* heroes provide that boost in a way that real men can't. Edward and Jacob have Bella up on a dizzyingly high pedestal. They tell her how wonderful she is. They show by their willingness to die for her just how important she is. It is nourishment for her hungry ego. Sadly, real men don't usually provide this kind of validation.

There is part of us that would love the type of attention that

Bella gets. Women have egos, just like men. We girls often laugh at male vanity and say 'typical man'. And it is true to a certain extent. Studies of men's and women's conversations show that men are far likelier to brag and boast. Girls think of themselves as more sensible and unassuming. We behave modestly. We don't go around boasting about how wonderful we are.

On the face of it, it looks as if women's egos aren't the same as men's. But this is wrong – our egos just manifest themselves in a different way. We don't care so much whether we are the best at sports or have the most expensive car. But we want a man to see we are the most special, loveable person in the world.

Most girls believe they deserve to have a man fall deeply in love with them. We feel it's our birthright. And why should a man fall in love with us? Because we are special and unique, of course. Deep down, most girls think sooner or later a man will see that and fall deeply in love with them. They hope a man will see how amazing they are underneath and because of this will feel an overwhelming, long-lasting love. If the boyfriend's feelings fade and they go off with another woman, it is because there is something wrong with the man, not them. If a man could only properly see how special they were, then they would be truly loved.

Bella gets this from Edward. We want this, too.

6) The thrill of the predator/prey relationship

Jacob and Edward are predators. They hunt animals and kill them for food. Edward is like a lion and Jacob is a wolf. Your emotions are primed to respond to predators. The first emotion Bella felt for Edward was a 'thrill' of fear.

Picture this and notice how your emotions respond:

> *You're walking through the hot African savannah. You are alone and thirsty, and have to find water soon. At last*

you find a watering hole amongst the dense grass. You sense someone hidden is staring at you but when you look around there is nothing. You bend down to drink. A tiny sound of a leaf rustling makes you spin round. Nothing. All is still, all is quiet. You wait, checking and rechecking. It's safe. You drink again.

Suddenly your instincts blaze with fear. You spring up. A lion crouches behind you, ready to pounce. You run. You feel the hot breath of the lion against the back of your neck. It's upon you. You feel the piercing agony as his teeth sink into your soft flesh. The last thing you hear in your short life is the snapping sound as his jaws crush your spine.

The fear of being eaten is laid down deep in your brain. That's one of the reasons why you find vampires fascinating. Predators that might eat you cause huge reactions in your nervous system, and the thought of being bitten triggers off a whole load of activity in the emotional parts of your brain. Vampires are similar to a big predator like a lion, but in human form.

Plenty of nonsense has been written about *Twilight* and other vampire stories, much of it along these lines: 'You love vampires because the threat of being bitten by one represents your unconscious, repressed longings and fears about sexual intercourse... blah blah blah.'

Some people, influenced by Sigmund Freud's ideas, think you're so afraid of your longings for sex that you'd rather think about being bitten instead, and being pierced by a fang is symbolic of the sexual act. This is nonsense. In modern life, longings for sex aren't repressed. You only have to see one or two Lady Gaga videos to know that. And neither are we particularly scared of sex. Some people (probably mostly men) would like to believe girls are terrified at the thought of the male sexual organ. But times have moved on. We're not, and it no longer makes sense to believe we love vampires because of some convoluted theory about repressed desire and the unconscious. Always be careful of people who try to tell you one thing is a symbol for something else. They can make up anything they like and there's no way of proving them right or wrong.

The fear of being bitten isn't a symbolic fear of sex. It is a fear of being bitten. There's nothing symbolic about it. If you're eaten, you die. You don't want to be somebody's prey.

For thousands of years human beings were caught up in this ancient battle of predator against prey. Facing danger and taking risks was something we endured every day. Now, in developed societies, there are very few predators in daily life, there are very few chases and thrills. You did not evolve to live quietly, and so you're drawn to excitement and danger in a story, even if you want a quiet life in reality. Your nervous system wasn't made for today's health and safety culture. In today's society all risks are managed. The most dangerous thing that might happen to you in a typical week is burning your tongue on a Pop-Tart.

In fiction and movies you might well enjoy scary things. Because you're safely curled up in your bed with a book or nestled in a cinema with a box of popcorn, you don't feel true fear, just a sense of excitement. Feeling scared but at the same time knowing you're pretty safe is a thrill. It's fun to be excited. Because Edward and Jacob are not real, you can safely enjoy the idea of danger from the comfort of your own home. You are drawn to excitement in your fictional men, in the same way you love to watch a thrilling car chase in a movie.

The power and aggression of Edward and Jacob is scary, but because they are also physically attractive we feel excitement, rather than the urge to run. Studies show that when you're with an attractive person of the opposite sex and you feel scared, for example when on a roller coaster, the attraction is stronger. When fear makes your heart beat faster you feel more attracted to that person.

When Bella is with the *Twilight* heroes she feels the ancient stirrings of the thrill of the predator/prey relationship. And you feel it, too.

7) Your urge to nurture

As a female you're prone to have a very caring side to your nature; this instinct is vital to ensuring that you would take care of any children that you have. When you see someone who is suffering or helpless, you are likely to feel compassion and want to help them. You get satisfaction from helping someone grow or heal. You're also more likely than a man to work in a caring profession. Although this area is controversial, psychologist Simon Baron-Cohen in his book *The Essential Difference* argues that nature has generally equipped women with better empathic instincts.

Both Edward and Jacob have compelling stories of suffering and inner turmoil. Love, tender care and compassion can soothe and heal them. Your nurturing side is hooked.

TO PUT IT IN A NUTSHELL

You love the *Twilight* heroes because they provide unconditional devotion, are stunningly handsome, exciting, powerful men, who make the object of their affections feel like the most desirable woman in the world. Only she can truly understand them and make them whole. It is a combination that is hard to resist.

And that's not all they do...

CHAPTER 3

TWILIGHT: THE ULTIMATE ROMANCE

THE DIFFERENCE BETWEEN LOVE AND ROMANCE

Love is an eternal emotion, and it has been around forever.

But what about romance? When do you think romance began?

The answer may surprise you. Romance was only invented a few centuries ago. Romance is all about putting love on a pedestal, seeing love as an exalted state, the path to exquisite happiness and pain. Romance is being in love with the idea of love, seeing love in an idealised way. The first romantic stories were all about the desperate, hopeless love of a knight for a high-born lady, a woman he could never attain. Known as 'courtly love' in medieval times, this adoration from afar was seen as the romantic ideal. Over the centuries, our ideal of love has changed.

Modern women dream of experiencing the ultimate romance for themselves; of finding a wonderful guy to make them happy. Everywhere you look there are songs and stories about true love. Most girls today hope to fall in love and live happily ever after.

It hasn't always been like this.

Until around the nineteenth century, the ordinary woman didn't expect to fall in love and live happily ever after. The people that chose your partner would be your parents, and the matches were made for mainly financial reasons. Arranged marriages still happen all over the world where females have little economic power. It was only when women began to have money of their own that they were able to marry for love. People in the past didn't base their lives and happiness around love. They didn't look for personal fulfilment from it in the same way as today. But nowadays many people believe that finding love is the path to happiness. This idea has been endorsed and perpetuated by romantic fiction.

Centuries ago, a 'romance' was a very unrealistic tale of adventure, often in an enchanted setting or featuring monsters, fairies or witches – romances were not tales of love. The stories typically focused on the adventures of a hero as he fought to win a fair maiden, but there was no emphasis on the development of their relationship.

In the present, the only story we call a 'romance' is a love story, so modern romantic fiction has its roots in the tradition of telling unrealistic, idealised stories.

✱ A HISTORY OF THE ROMANTIC NOVEL ✱

The first romantic novel, as we recognise it today, was called *Pamela, or Virtue Rewarded* by Samuel Richardson, published in 1740, the story of a servant girl who falls in love with and eventually marries her master. It was the first book to be written from the woman's point of view and to focus on the love relationship. Then in 1813, Jane Austen's *Pride and Prejudice* was published and became one of the most popular love stories ever. With *Jane Eyre* and *Wuthering Heights* in 1847, the Brontë sisters produced love stories with a dark, Gothic feel, similar in mood to the *Twilight* series. *Jane Eyre*, *Wuthering Heights* and *Twilight* are love stories which include the Gothic elements of horror, madness, the supernatural, and brooding male characters who both frighten and fascinate.

The first historical romance came out in 1921, *The Black Moth* by Georgette Heyer. As society changed and women became more liberated, historical romances became sexier and the 'bodice-ripper' became popular, the first one being *The Flame and the Flower* by

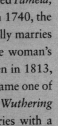

Kathleen Woodiwiss, published in 1972. In 1980, publishers were even more daring and produced the first line of romantic novels which didn't require the heroine to be a virgin. The first of these was *The Tawny Gold Man* by Amii Lorin. The modern chick lit type love story was born in 1996 with *Bridget Jones's Diary* by Helen Fielding. These stories have independent, funny heroines who are much more open and frank about their sex lives.

All love stories are similar: boy meets girl, there are obstacles, love is powerful enough to overcome these obstacles, and in the end they live happily ever after. Our taste for romantic stories with happy endings has become stronger and stronger. Traditionally, fairy tales were grim and dark. By the nineteenth century, old fairy tales were rewritten to become romantic tales with happy endings. An early version of the *Sleeping Beauty* story was written in 1634 by Giambattista Basile. It is about a girl who pricks her finger on a poisoned splinter and falls into a deep sleep. A prince, who is already married to someone else, comes along, sees the sleeping girl and rapes her while she's unconscious. She then gives birth to twins and wakes up when one of the twins suckles the poisoned splinter from her finger. The prince's wife is angry with his adultery so she steals the twins and plans to have them cooked and fed to the prince. The prince finds out about her plot, throws his wife on the fire, leaving him free to marry the sleeping beauty.

Over the centuries, the story was retold by other writers, who changed elements of the plot. In 1812 the Brothers Grimm ended the story when the (single and eligible!) prince wakes Sleeping Beauty with a gentle kiss. They get married immediately – but there is no mention of her falling in love with him first. In the 1959 Disney version, the plot is changed once again, to cater for the modern appetite for romance and happy endings. This time

Sleeping Beauty has already met the prince and fallen in love with him before she falls asleep.

TWILIGHT – THE CLASSIC LOVE STORY

Twilight is a new version of the classic love story, where the heroine's love transforms and redeems the dark hero.

Edward and Jacob – dark heroes

Characters like Edward and Jacob have appeared in love stories throughout the centuries. We are drawn to this type of man time and again. This is the 'dark hero', like Heathcliff in *Wuthering Heights*, or Mr Rochester in *Jane Eyre*; a man who is domineering, arrogant, rebellious, struggles with dark impulses, is moody, an outcast and enigmatic.

In romantic stories, we adore the dark hero because we know he is a loving, passionate tender partner underneath, and that he can be transformed or redeemed and made to show his true nature through the power of his love for the heroine.

Edward Cullen

Edward is the ultimate dark hero. At the beginning of the story he is aggressive, unsmiling and aloof. He is always 'piercing' Bella with his powerful gaze. He is hostile to Bella. He drives extremely fast, a risk taker. He is tortured by his own dark impulses. He feels deeply alone and sad. In the *Twilight* story, we discover Edward is not 'dark' really. Through the love affair with Bella, we discover he is gentle and kind underneath. We learn that he has been waiting 90 years for her to be born and has never as much as looked at another woman. He conquers his murderous impulses towards Bella and the problems are solved. His love for Bella changes him.

By the end of the saga he's turned into an ideal husband and father. He commits to loving Bella forever, and provides her with perfect love.

Jacob Black

At the start of *Twilight*, Jacob doesn't seem to be a dark hero. He's eager to please Bella and is friendly, cooperative and safe. Then she discovers he is a shape-shifter and capable of terrible aggression. He becomes more domineering and forces a kiss from Bella. Far from being harmless and easy to please, he becomes increasingly brooding, dark and angry. He is tortured by his existence as a werewolf. He is a lethal fighter. He becomes a 'dark hero' as well. But we know his love for Bella makes him kind and a good person underneath.

Why do you adore the 'dark hero'?

The brooding, dangerous hero, who is really a great guy underneath, appeals to your deepest instincts. Psychology research has shown that guys can be divided into two basic types in the way they court women. The first type is known as the 'cad'. We know them in our everyday lives as 'bad boys'. The bad boy has dominant body language – he has a proud, upright posture, he makes bold eye contact with people, smiles rarely and can be rebellious. He tends to take risks, and is brave and aggressive. He is not afraid of confrontation. He is competitive. He is not the settling down type. He doesn't like to be tied to one woman. He is likely to flit from girl to girl. He can't be relied on to support his children.

The other main kind of man is the 'good dad'. We know them as the 'nice guy'. This type of man is ideal husband and father material. The 'nice guy' is hard-working, sensitive and kind. He is not aggressive and doesn't take risks. He likes to cooperate with you rather than be domineering. He doesn't look at other women and is faithful and committed. He will stick by you and provide for his children.

These two types of men have been around for thousands of years. 'Bad boy' tactics succeed in producing offspring, because he gets many women pregnant. The 'nice guy' doesn't have as many children, but he will look after them well. You are wired to respond to these two main courtship strategies. You find the bad boy exciting and attractive, but you also want a decent guy.

This is a contradiction that successful novel writers play on – in romantic fiction you can have them both. They deliberately create a character who is the classic 'dark hero': a bad boy and a nice guy at the same time, a difficult, dangerous man who is really a loving, tender, faithful partner underneath.

Stephenie Meyer knows how to appeal to the female heart. She has created romantic heroes who combine everything we want. They are the perfect mixture. We are attracted to a dominant, rebellious, powerful, unpredictable, complicated man, AND a loving, sensitive, faithful one. Edward is both. Jacob is both. We find this satisfying. We can have our cake and eat it.

Do you prefer a 'bad boy' or a 'nice guy'?

You might be more attracted to one type than the other.

Read about these two different guys and notice how you respond to them:

Daniel takes you to a country pub on the back of his motorbike. He drives fast and you have to close your eyes tight as he leans the bike into the corners. He strides into the pub and puts his hand on the small of your back as he steers you to a seat. He talks about his latest rock-climbing expedition and his plans to hitchhike around the world. His gaze is straight and piercing. There aren't many seats in the bar, and another guy comes towards you and gestures towards a seat next to you. There is a space, but it would mean you'd be cramped. Daniel shakes his head and frowns, and the guy backs off. A pretty girl walks past and you notice his eyes flicker towards her curvy figure.

Ben drives you to a country pub. He drives sensibly and you feel safe with him. He walks with you to the bar and asks where you would like to sit. He keeps a respectful distance as you find your seats. He talks about his latest hiking expedition and his plans to train as a teacher. His gaze is non-threatening. There are not many seats at the bar and another guy comes towards you and gestures enquiringly towards the spare seat. There is a space, but it would mean you'd be cramped. Ben nods and says, that's fine, we can make room. A pretty girl walks past and Ben doesn't seem to notice.

Who do you prefer?
In fact, it's a bit of a trick question. You might well have liked the sound of both. They both appeal to women.

However, some women have a clear preference for one or the other, preferring Daniel or Ben. Bella is strongly attracted to a 'bad boy'. She is turned off by the eager-to-please Mike, Tyler and Eric. She doesn't feel particularly attracted to Jacob at first, when he is the straightforward, friendly guy. But she is attracted to him more when she finds out about his dark side.

TWILIGHT TAKES IT FURTHER

Although Edward and Jacob are the classic dark heroes over whom women have swooned for centuries, they take the fantasy to the next level. They are not only the perfect blend of exciting bad boy and loving nice guy, but they have a whole load of other superhuman qualities. With Edward's diamond skin, Jacob's shape-shifting and their immortality, they reach new extremes.

The new romantic heroes, Edward and Jacob, have lost any relation to reality. The *Twilight* heroes make traditional heroes like Heathcliff, Romeo and Mr Darcy look a bit... well... bleh.

In a way, this is what modern men have done in their fantasies of women; they fantasise about women who do not bear much relation to reality. Surgical enhancements, botox and airbrushing have created an ideal that isn't attainable.

But we women dream about more than just appearance. We have taken the fantasy up yet another notch. We want even more from our dream guys...

Chapter 4

Edward and Jacob Are Gods and You Need Them Now!

A man is no longer enough

In our fantasies now, we want more than just a man. We want a god!

Jacob and Edward are like young deities walking on the earth. They are both immortal. They have superhuman strength and powers. Jacob can change himself into a wolf at will, Edward can read minds. They are both incredibly powerful protectors for Bella. They both offer eternal, unconditional love. Edward can grant you everlasting life. They have qualities that are more divine than human.

Human beings have a need for a god or gods to worship. We realise how fragile, weak and mortal we are, and crave a powerful protector who will watch over us and grant us eternal life. You're drawn to Edward and Jacob because they fulfil your human longing for a god. Ancient peoples often worshipped gods that were part animal and part human, like Edward and Jacob. One of the oldest statues in the world, more than thirty thousand years old, is a figure that is half lion, half human (known as the lion man of the Hohlenstein Stadel); the ancient Egyptians had an array of hybrid gods, and the part-elephant god Ganesh is worshipped by Hindus today.

In years to come, when people read *Twilight* to try to understand our society, they might assume that Edward and Jacob were part of a religion. Some fans actually believe this to be true:

> *Casey is 17 years old and makes a point of reading extracts from the* Twilight *books every day, as if they were the Bible. She has the red-edged special edition of the books which she keeps wrapped up in a gold cloth under her bed. She calls herself a Cullenist. She wants to go on a pilgrimage to Forks for her eighteenth birthday. She believes that Stephenie Meyer is a prophet, and that the Cullen family is real.*

You probably don't take it this far, but Edward the vampire is compelling because he can make you forever young and beautiful. Most of us don't like to think about ageing and dying; if anything, it is repressed in our society. It's about accepting that one day we will die and we can't know for sure what, if anything, happens afterwards. Many young people do not have a strong belief in an afterlife, so they have to face their own mortality without the comfort that a deep-seated faith brings. This is part of the fascination of the *Twilight* saga, as it deals with our own human fears of ageing and death. *Twilight* is not just about love, it is about dying. Throughout the series, Bella faces her own death and that of her loved ones. On her eighteenth birthday it hits her that she will become old, die and never see Edward again. Bella longs for him to change her so she can become inhumanly beautiful, live forever and have eternal love.

Twilight gives us a fantasy world where we can be forever young. We share Bella's fears about ageing, dying and being parted from our loved ones. Human beings have always dreamed of an afterlife but *Twilight* gives us an alternative. With one bite, Edward the vampire can grant us everlasting life. Edward can fulfil the desire that we share with all living creatures: our longing to cheat death.

LONGING FOR LOVE

Edward and Jacob provide the type of love you dream about. It is eternal, profound and unconditional. It is irresistible to the twenty-first-century woman, because in today's world we crave love more than ever.

As a young woman in the West in the twenty-first century you are told you should strive to be independent, but your nature is telling you differently. You are likely to be living amongst strangers, but you are human and you need to have close bonds with people. Being alone is not a comfortable state for most. For thousands of years humans lived together in small groups. The natural way of living is to interact with people you know intimately, whose future is tightly bound up with your own. In the past, your survival depended on it. Loneliness was unheard of in ancient times. A woman who went off on her own soon died from hunger or thirst, or was eaten by predators.

But today, loneliness is an epidemic amongst the old and young alike.

YOUNG AND ALONE

A recent survey showed that young people are likelier to feel lonely than older people. In the West, living closely with others is frowned upon, unless you are a couple with dependent children. Children who grow up but never leave home are jeered at. Couples who invite their elderly mothers or fathers to live with them are looked at with sympathy and advised to put them in a care home. You would be seen as odd to have your aunt or cousin set up home with you.

It's difficult to keep a friend for life now. They move to the other side of the country or the world for work or study. They meet other people, find someone they like better than you, and you drift apart. It's not necessarily easy for you to make new friends in today's crowded but anonymous cities, and when you meet someone new, they may not be particularly interested in bonding with you, yet another stranger.

In ancient cultures, friendships were seen as the most important relationships in your life. The Romans used to think love between men was the most sacred and valuable love you could experience. Stories and poems were written about the close bond between warriors. Friendship was an eternal contract. But today, friendship is not seen as the be-all and end-all. You are expected to move around many different social groups, breaking and making new friendships.

Today, the love between a man and a woman is upheld as the most important, valuable, profound experience of your life. The couple is seen as the basic unit of society. Love and eventually marriage is seen as the way to fulfil your need for intimacy. So this becomes your focus. Many girls will put up with a bad relationship with a boyfriend because it's better than being alone.

Eighteen-year-old Ros was excited about moving to London to study. But after a couple of months she realised there was something missing. Even though she was surrounded by people, she felt she couldn't connect with anyone.

'Everyone around me seemed to have busy lives of their own. I'd been looking forward to being independent, as I saw myself as a modern young woman who could rely on myself. But I just felt incredibly lonely, day after day.'

That's why she rushed into a relationship with Chris.

He had picked her up at the student bar, and from the beginning she sensed he would not be good for her. He was a restless and dissatisfied person. She could tell by the way he glanced at other women all the time that he was not the committed type.

But anything was better than loneliness, so she turned a blind eye to the signs that he was never going to be a good boyfriend. Sure enough, after a few months she found out he had been cheating on her all along.

The craving for love is one of the reasons we adore romantic fiction. Over half of all the books sold are love stories. We have an enormous appetite for tales of true love. We cannot get enough of pop songs about love, or romantic comedies on film and TV.

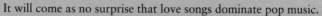

✶ LOVE IS ALL AROUND YOU ✶

It will come as no surprise that love songs dominate pop music.

Sociologists have analysed the pop charts across the decades, adding up how many songs deal with love and heartbreak. They've found that 73 per cent of pop songs are about romantic love.

Interestingly, this proportion has not changed much over time, despite changing musical tastes. Go back to the music of the 1930s and you'll still find three-quarters of popular songs are love songs.

The form has changed, though. In the 1930s, love songs were almost always ballads. And nearly all popular songs for female singers were about love. Modern music is more diverse – a study by the University of Colorado found 96 per cent of rhythm and blues songs were about love, 82 per cent of rock and roll but only 59 per cent of rap and hip hop. But the trend for female singers singing more love songs than male pop stars has remained.

The song rated as having the most words about love per line is the duet 'Endless Love' by Diana Ross and Lionel Richie.

Bella was extremely lonely when she moved to Forks. She had no one she could turn to. She was not close to anyone, not even her own father. She cried on her own, and kept her pain to herself. She was a typical product of modern life, wrenched from the environment she was familiar with and forced to go through the discomfort of being judged by a new social group. Then the relationship with Edward changed everything. She was no longer lonely.

Reading about love is enjoyable but it does not satisfy your desire for love. *It makes your desire stronger*. And the *Twilight* series is one of the most compelling love stories in the world.

LOVE HURTS

You want love but know it can be a rocky path; you may have been hurt yourself. So you draw inspiration and comfort from reading about it in a story. You feel a connection with Bella's sufferings (even if you're also mad with her for complaining when she has the most gorgeous, wonderful Edward! And Jacob!).

Everyone knows that, although love is a wonderful thing, it can also be the most painful experience of your life. If you see a girl crying, you can bet that nine times out of ten it's because of a guy. Having your heart broken is devastating, and that's why many of us are eager to read love stories, to see how the heroine works out her romantic problems and have that satisfying ending where true love conquers all.

We are fascinated by love stories because we know how complicated and difficult it is to find the right man. Millions of women are hurt and disappointed in love because they have chosen a boyfriend who is not right for them. If you had an unhappy childhood, you might be particularly vulnerable to ending up with the wrong man. For example, girls who have suffered violence in the home as a child are often drawn towards aggressive men because intimacy and violence is familiar to them. Other negative experiences in childhood, such as excessive criticism or bullying, can lead to low self-esteem and make a woman more likely to settle for a man they feel they deserve, rather than the type of man they want and can be happy with. But even those who have had the most loving backgrounds are not immune to relationship difficulties.

In fact, happy, healthy young women fall in love on the flimsiest basis with men totally unsuited to them. Most of us have done it at one time or another. The divorce rate speaks for itself; about half of marriages end in divorce, and not all lasting marriages are happy. Finding the right man is often a difficult, pain-strewn path. In *Twilight*, Bella simply pitches up to her new school and her ideal soulmate is there sitting next to her on the same desk. Imagine moving to a new school/college/job to find your Edward or Jacob just sitting there waiting for you. If only!

TWILIGHT – THE ESCAPE FROM THE REALITY OF TWENTY-FIRST-CENTURY MEN

If you look beneath the glitter of Edward's skin and put aside the shape-shifting, blood-sucking elements of the story, *Twilight* is strangely old-fashioned. Bella and Edward are both virgins until they marry. There is no expectation of casual sex. Bella settles happily into her role as wife and, later, mother. There is no mention of Bella having a career.

This was how love stories looked years ago, before your great-grandmother was born. But society has changed – women are expected to have jobs and careers, to look after themselves financially and sex before marriage is seen as the norm.

Once the contraceptive pill was invented and women were free to have sex without fear of pregnancy, some people predicted a future where women could indulge in casual sex if they liked, without being judged. People hoped there would be equality between men and women with regard to their sex lives.

It hasn't worked out like that, though.

> *After a painful split from her last boyfriend and a couple of short-term flings while on the rebound, Kirsty didn't want to rush into another serious relationship. She decided to take her time to get to know the next guy. So when she started seeing men seriously she didn't want to get physical too soon. She went out with Jordan, a guy she'd liked for ages, and after she explained this to him he never contacted her again. She found out later he'd told his mates he went out with her because he'd heard she'd sleep with anyone.*

What does the modern man have to offer you? All too often, it seems the answer is – not a lot. He may well expect sex on a casual basis, he doesn't necessarily expect to commit to you and he certainly doesn't expect to support you financially.

These days, many men expect to have sex, even in the most casual and uncommitted of relationships. You may be wondering whether this works for you; many girls are finding short-term flings are not really what they want. And decades of perceived equality have not changed the fact that girls are judged for having casual sex whereas guys are not.

One of the downsides of being more equal to guys is that the old-fashioned deference and respect for girls has gone.

VAMPIRES KNOW HOW TO TREAT A WOMAN

Jasper Hale, the husband of Alice Cullen, was an officer in the Confederate States Army during the American Civil War. On the last night of his human life, he was politely reverent to the evil vampire Maria and her companions in the moments before she attacked him. All his life he had been brought up to respect women, and to protect them because they were considered the weaker sex. In the era he was brought up, and Edward, too, love-making was seen as something special within marriage. Casual sex was deeply wrong and not respectful to a woman. Pressurising a woman for sex was considered to be ungentlemanly conduct.

Guys aren't brought up with these social mores nowadays. Today pictures of scantily clad celebrities fill the daily papers and pornography is freely available on the Internet. Young men are being conditioned to believe that women are sexual playthings.

The *Twilight* vampires offer old-fashioned devotion and commitment. We are nostalgic for what seems a more romantic age, where the physical bond between a man and a woman is sacred. When Edward proposes to Bella and refuses to sully their love by getting physical without the holy bond of matrimony, we sigh. Why can't real men be like that?

TWILIGHT – AN ESCAPE FROM THE REALITY OF BEING A TWENTY-FIRST-CENTURY WOMAN

Maybe you have seen your mother struggle with a job and children and it's not an appealing prospect.

Jamila is a 22-year-old medical student. Her parents have sacrificed a huge amount so she can study. Coming from poverty themselves, it was their dream to give their daughter the opportunities they didn't have.

But Jamila is finding it hard. She works long into the night and is treated like dirt by the senior doctors. She is at breaking point after being yelled at by a senior consultant in front of a patient for getting a medical term wrong. She can't see an end to it. When she qualifies as a junior doctor, she'll have to work even harder and have far more responsibilities. One day she'd like to have a family, but she has seen how hard it is for the older female doctors. The long, unsocial hours just don't fit with being a mother of young children.

She is in love with Ali, a newly qualified doctor who tells her she should give up her studies if she hates it that much. He says that they can live together and he will support her.

Jamila is tempted, but she is terrified of letting her parents down. It was their lifelong hope that their child would become a modern, independent career woman. How can she shatter their dreams?

One of the reasons *Twilight* might attract you now is that it is an enticingly simple alternative. Finding a loving man who will look after you seems alluring compared to the complexity of competing at work, struggling to get qualifications and the ball and chain of the nine-to-five existence. Women have fought for these 'freedoms' but, to many, they don't look that great. Why not just find a wonderful guy who can support you financially? It sounds tempting. Especially if the man in question is Edward.

SECRET ONE: SUMMARY

The *Twilight* heroes are irresistible because:

- They offer unconditional love.
- They are beautiful.
- They are perfect hunters.
- They are warriors.
- They do wonders for their girlfriend's self-esteem.
- They are 'bad boys' who are really 'nice guys'.

- They are exciting predators.
- They have compelling stories of suffering.
- They are like gods.
- They solve the dilemmas of the woman living in the twenty-first century.

So far, it all sounds good, doesn't it? Read on to hear about the dangers.

Discover the Hidden Dangers of Your Romantic Imagination

(You have romance on the brain!)

CHAPTER 5

TWILIGHT AND YOUR LOVE LIFE

The path to true love is strewn with perils for the unwary. And romantic fiction like *Twilight* is so powerful that it might influence the type of guy you choose.

AN UNEXPECTED SECRET

Who do you think does the picking and choosing in relationships, the man or the woman?

Ask a man, and they'll say it's them. They tend to be the ones who ask women out or make the first move. In their minds, they are in control.

But the truth may surprise you. Studies show that girls do most of the choosing in relationships. And women are most likely to end relationships – it is usually the woman, not the man, who files for divorce.

Research has revealed that although it is guys who make the first approach, they are responding to non-verbal signals women give out. So when a guy chats you up, it's actually you making the first move, but you are doing it at a non-verbal level.

 SPEAKING WITHOUT WORDS

The basics of body language are widely known. If you want a guy to come over and start talking to you, your primary signal will be eye contact – gazing at him for a few seconds, looking down when he notices, and then repeating. This is unmistakable, and a guy instinctively knows you are saying, 'I might be interested in you, it's worth approaching me.'

Then there are the other signals in your ammunition locker: playing with your hair or the hair flick; tilting your head to one side to show your face and neck in a vulnerable way; and self-touching, for example brushing your collarbone, fiddling with accessories, leaning towards a guy.

Once you start talking, it will be long gazes into his eyes that indicate to a man that you like him and you might say yes if he asks you out. Other signals you give off include laughing enthusiastically at his jokes or talking animatedly or lowering the pitch of your voice. It's instinctive: if you like a guy, you will find yourself opening your body language and making demure sideways glances almost before you are consciously aware of your attraction to him.

Ever wondered why sometimes a guy asks you out or propositions you even though you have zero attraction to him? It might be that he's just chancing his luck – asking out multiple women per night in the expectation of rejections, but knowing occasionally he'll get a yes, just as spam emailers send out countless offers in return for the occasional hit. But it might well be because he has misread your signals – laughing at his joke, for example. What for you is a genuine laugh is for him a sign that you like him.

Girls are much choosier than men. You are the one who decides whether the relationship goes ahead or not.

So you are the one who chooses the boyfriend who breaks your heart. And romantic fiction like *Twilight* can steer you towards the type of guy who will break your heart and leave you devastated. You might think this is nonsense. After all, *Twilight* is only a story, right?

HOW STORIES CHANGE YOUR LIFE

People have always loved stories. They are a way of helping you make sense of reality and find out about life. Good stories grip your emotions and contain messages you take to heart.

Telling a story is a great way to change people's minds and influence their behaviour. It doesn't matter whether it is in a book or a film.

Here's an example: if someone told you to stop eating a certain food, you'd probably take no notice. But thousands of people stopped eating pork after watching *Babe*, the heart-warming children's film that tells the story of a cute piglet. If you bring something to life in an emotional story, then people take notice.

Throughout history, people have recognised the power of the written word. When *Lady Chatterley's Lover* first came out in 1928, a novel by D. H. Lawrence about a woman who has an adulterous affair with a gamekeeper, it could not be published in Britain because of its explicit descriptions of sex. Men everywhere were worried that their wives and daughters would read the book and be inspired to follow suit.

Books and films can change your beliefs, and your beliefs change your behaviour. The power of human belief is the driving force behind the most wonderful and the most terrible of human acts – the belief that man could fly drove us to discover the miracle of air travel, and yet the power of belief drove terrorists to crash two aeroplanes into the World Trade Center.

Because of modern technology you are exposed to far more stories than ever before. In ancient times, you would have been limited to hearing tales around the campfire. There would only be a handful of people around with a stock of good stories. You'd have gathered round in the evening, and Grandma Ugg would start on a tale handed down from her ancestors and you would groan, 'Oh Grandma, not that old story of how the Great Warrior

Ogg forgot his flint axe one day and got cornered by a pack of wolves that bit him on the bum. Yeah, yeah – we get it; forget the flint axe and you'll regret it.'

But now your exposure to stories is almost infinite due to limitless access to books, blogs, TV and films. Think of how much you read or see in your everyday life. If you're reading this, you probably adore books about love. How many books have you read? How many romantic films have you seen? These stories play a significant role in your decision-making and how you live your life. And *Twilight* is one of the most popular and powerful stories ever. At least 85 million people have read it worldwide, and countless more have watched the films. *Twilight* has captured your imagination and engaged your emotions like no other story has.

A powerful story like *Twilight* will affect your mind.

HOW CAN A STORY LEAD YOU INTO DANGER?

One theory is that you fall in love with a person you meet who fits your ideal fantasy. You fall in love with the story you weave around the real person, not the person themselves. That's why the beginning of the relationship is so exciting. You believe all your fantasies may be coming true. You have an image of the guy you dream about and you project this image on the man in front of you.

If you have a powerful imaginary love story like *Twilight* as your ideal, you will have an Edward- or Jacob-shaped hole in your life and your mind will distort your boyfriend so he will fit.

So *Twilight* has affected your brain. That's what great books and films do! They change how you see the world. But the powerful messages in *Twilight* may have affected your beliefs about men and love. Most people think 'romance' means a love affair, but the word has another meaning in the dictionary. It also means 'to tell extravagant or improbable lies' and 'romantic' means imaginary or fictitious. This is the problem with romantic fiction – it is made up. Romantic fiction is full of messages about love and human nature that are just plain wrong. Love stories follow the rules of romance, not the rules of real human psychology.

THE MOST DANGEROUS ROMANTIC RULES

In romantic fiction, men obey rules of behaviour that make for a satisfying love story.

✳ THE RULES OF ROMANTIC FICTION ✳

Love will change him.
Love will gentle him.
A violent man is a nice guy underneath.
If a man loves a woman, it makes up for his violent behaviour.

Both Edward and Jacob are dangerous. But because they fall in love, they turn into wonderful, gentle guys.

In *Twilight*, Edward is a tortured, hostile man who wants to kill Bella. By *Breaking Dawn* he is the ideal loving husband and father.

In *New Moon*, Jacob is an unpredictable, ferocious werewolf. In *Breaking Dawn*, he is a tender protector and ideal future husband for the child Renesmee.

Both of them are domineering and aggressive, but underneath they are sensitive, faithful lovers. Through their feelings for Bella they reveal their tender natures.

This makes a fantastic, enjoyable story.

But it is not real life. Real men don't follow the rules of romance. A dominant, aggressive, dangerous man is not a 'nice guy' waiting to happen.

Twilight leads you to believe that a man can thirst for your blood but at the same time be an ideal boyfriend, and that a man who can turn into an uncontrollable, savage wolf if he loses his temper is really a gentle guy.

But never forget this is fiction.

REALITY IS VERY DIFFERENT...

In reality, dangerous men do not make good boyfriends. Their love does not make them less dangerous to you, it makes them more dangerous. Predator and prey is not a good model for a blissful love life. In reality, when the lion lies down with the lamb, what happens afterwards is not positive for the lamb...

Twilight gives us more empathy for the sufferings of the tortured, disturbed man, and makes him seem a sympathetic character. It gives the impression that a dangerous predator could be ideal boyfriend material.

There are plenty of real-life human predators. And women fall in love with them all the time. A notorious example of a real-life predator is Richard Ramirez, a serial killer still in prison in California. He broke into people's homes and raped, tortured, mutilated and murdered his victims. He was likened to a vampire because he stalked people at night and was fascinated with blood. He was convicted of horrific, sadistic crimes. But Doreen Lioy, a magazine journalist, fell in love with him and married him in prison.

The press made much of the fact that Doreen was an educated woman, and that she should have known better. She had a degree in English literature. Yet when it came to judging Ramirez she was naive in the extreme. She was inexperienced sexually and a virgin, and truly believed that Ramirez was a wonderful guy. She managed to romanticise a notorious, sadistic killer. Her education didn't prevent her from doing this. It's possible that her exposure to romantic fiction may have even encouraged it.

THE ORDINARY AGGRESSIVE GUY

Luckily monsters like Ramirez are few and I hope you will never meet one. But you are still at risk from the more day-to-day aggressive guy.

If an aggressive man loves you it is dangerous, because love is not just about warm, tender feelings. Love can involve fear, jealousy and anger. If a dangerous man loves you, the negative emotions that are part of any intense relationship are likely to tip over into violence.

Sixteen-year-old schoolgirl Kat knew that her 19-year-old boyfriend Sam had a temper. He had a reputation for getting into fights. But when he was with her he was a different person. He could be really tender and passionate. He took her to a fair and won a massive teddy bear for her. He gave it to her and named it Sam, so she could cuddle it when they were apart and think of him. He reminded her of Jacob; dangerous, but incredibly warm and faithful. He never looked at another girl when she was with him. He told her she had changed him.

Kat had a friend from childhood called Nathan, a quiet guy with glasses who'd lived next door. She'd never fancied him, but they were friends and he came round one day to fix her computer. Sam arrived and when Nathan answered the door, Sam punched him to the ground. Kat screamed at him to stop and Sam slapped her in the face.

Kat made the mistake of thinking that love could calm and gentle a man. Sadly, this is not a psychological truth. A dominant, aggressive man cannot be loved and soothed out of his faults.

DON'T BE TOO ALARMED, BUT...

Choosing a boyfriend can be one of the riskiest decisions of your life. There is a sizeable minority of aggressive men. One in four British women will be assaulted by their partner or ex-partner at some point in their lives.

One incident of domestic violence is reported to the police every minute. Ninety per cent of domestic abuse on women occurs in the victim's own home. And, at the extreme, on average two women in Britain are killed every week by a current or former male partner.

For most victims of violence the outcome is not death or serious injury. The most common types of assault are pushing, pulling and grabbing, but slapping, kicking or hitting with fists accounts for nearly half of all incidents. Bruising is the most common injury a woman experiences, but one in ten cases results in cuts or broken bones.

The emotional damage caused by domestic violence outlives the bruises. It can last for years, tainting future relationships.

Whilst these statistics are worrying, the majority of men will never inflict this sort of damage on you. It's important to remember that 75 per cent of women will not suffer domestic abuse at any time during their lives.

THE TRUTH ABOUT HUMAN BEHAVIOUR

Psychology has revealed many things about human beings. But the most consistent finding – a truth that comes up again and again – is something very simple:

The best way to predict how someone will behave in the future is to look at the pattern of how they have behaved in the past.

It's as easy as that.

Psychologists have drawn up questionnaires which predict how risky a person is. And how do they do it? They look at the person's past behaviour patterns. It's the most reliable method.

That is the rule in real life. People do not change easily. They do not change just because someone loves them. If you spot a man who is showing signs of aggression, you can predict he will behave like this in the future.

But the romantic rule in stories like *Twilight* leads readers to believe that signs of danger are just a prelude to your man transforming into the perfect lover, or that really he's a nice guy underneath. The trouble with romantic fiction is it's all about how people change. Yet the psychological reality is people are far more likely to stay the same.

ROMANTIC LOVE – THE GREAT REDEEMER?

Another idea in romantic fiction is that a guy can behave in terrible ways, but if he loves a woman, then he is redeemed. In other words, his capacity to love somehow makes up for all his bad behaviour. This is the message Bella takes from *Wuthering Heights*. Bella admits Heathcliff is a nasty piece of work. In the story he hangs his bride's pet dog on their wedding night, starves and terrorises his dying son and punches Catherine's daughter in the face. Yet Bella believes his passion for Catherine lifts him up and almost excuses him.

No one should be surprised that bad men can fall in love. Human beings, no matter how evil, are wired to form attachments to others. Violent, unpleasant men are capable of love, like anyone else. When they love a woman, they usually love her in a violent, unpleasant way. Heathcliff was just following his own essential nature. He wasn't doing anything noble or good by loving Catherine. He was just instinctively experiencing his own ugly brand of passion. Disappointed in love because Catherine married someone else, he devoted the rest of his life to making everyone as miserable as possible. Heathcliff mocks his wife Isabella's romantic delusions. He sneers at her for thinking he is 'a hero of romance' despite all the evidence of his brutality.

Some of the most evil men in history have fallen in love. Should we be led to believe this goes any way towards absolving them of their crimes?

DANGEROUS MEN IN HISTORY WHO HAVE LOVED

Henry VIII: was said to have loved five out of his six wives. The two he was thought to have loved most were Anne Boleyn and Catherine Howard. He had both of them beheaded.

Joseph Stalin: was responsible for at least 20 million deaths. He loved his first wife, saying 'she was very sweet and beautiful, she melted my heart'. He was so distraught when she died that at the funeral he threw himself into her grave on top of her coffin.

Adolf Hitler: ordered the murder of six million innocent men, women and children. He had passionate feelings for Eva Braun. He bought her a book of poetry, inscribed with love. He married her in a romantic gesture the day before their joint suicide.

Charles Manson: murdered at least nine people, and boasted that he was responsible for at least 35 killings. He was married twice, and wrote a love song called 'Cease to Exist' that was later adapted and recorded by the Beach Boys as 'Never Learn Not to Love'.

THE DIFFICULT, UNHAPPY GUY

You may be thinking the previous section doesn't apply to you, that you'd never be attracted to a guy with a violent temper. But there are other romantic pitfalls:

- Love will make an unhappy man into a happy one.
- Your love can cure him of his personal difficulties.

In romantic fiction, the hero is often aloof, mysterious, unsmiling and difficult. He has a secret sorrow and a tortured, unhappy soul. He dislikes the human race. But because of the heroine's love he is transformed into a wonderful, fulfilled partner. His unhappiness vanishes. They live happily ever after. This is the theme of countless love stories, including *Twilight*. Edward's pain and sadness is solved because of Bella. Jacob's unhappiness disappears once he imprints on Renesmee. The initial moodiness, difficulties and complexities of the man are just obstacles to be overcome by love, a prelude to the happy-ever-after.

In reality, love is not the solution for personal unhappiness. A difficult, moody guy will be a difficult, moody boyfriend. If you stick with him he will be a difficult, moody husband, and then, likely as not, he will be a difficult, moody ex-husband. This is the psychological reality of personality. People don't change who they are just because they are loved.

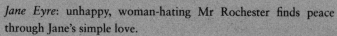

✷ DIFFICULT MEN IN ROMANTIC FICTION ✷ WHO ARE TRANSFORMED BY LOVE

Jane Eyre: unhappy, woman-hating Mr Rochester finds peace through Jane's simple love.

Pride and Prejudice: cold, contemptuous Mr Darcy is transformed into the perfect husband by his love for Elizabeth.

Rebecca: the heroine melts the icy heart of the tortured Maxim de Winter.

Beauty and the Beast: miserable, bitter Beast is turned into a handsome prince by the power of love.

THE INCOMPATIBLE GUY

 THE ROMANTIC RULES

Love will make incompatible people into compatible ones.
Love conquers all.

One of the most popular types of love story is when opposites fall in love and resolve their differences. One half of the couple transforms who they are because of their love for their partner. In *Breaking Dawn*, Bella transforms into a vampire to make her compatible with Edward. This is fine in a story, but in real life people can't – and usually don't want to – transform who they are.

> *Beth was attracted to Matt because he was her opposite. While Beth was restless, energetic and nervous, Matt was laid-back. She loved his calm, tranquil attitude. Beth was stressed from studying for an MBA while working full-time. Matt was working part-time in a surfing shop. She marvelled at the way he could spend the whole day just lying on the beach, thinking about life and connecting with nature. It was a real antidote to her frenetic lifestyle. He'd dropped out of uni and said he was escaping from the rat race for a year, just to be himself. She admired him for this.*
>
> *A year later Matt decided he enjoyed the easy life so much that he was going to continue it indefinitely. By this time, Beth had qualified and had been promoted. But she resented having to pay for everything. And Beth*

discovered that Matt's laid-back attitude extended to personal hygiene. He didn't wash his clothes or himself as much as she would have liked. When she pressured him to shower more, they argued. When she complained about paying for everything he sulked. Beth was full of pent-up energy – she wanted to travel the world, buy a house and rise up the ladder at work. Matt was happy pottering on his own bit of beach.

While lying on the sand one day Matt met Layla. Beth was at a high-powered business meeting. Layla was a laid-back surfer girl with relaxed ideas about personal grooming very like himself. They fell in love. He ended his relationship with Beth, in a typical casual fashion, by leaving a mumbled message on her mobile.

Beth had hoped that if she stuck around, she could make it work, just like in the movies. She saw their differences as obstacles to be overcome. She saw herself as the heroine in her own love story, where the hero sees her true worth in the end and the bond of love overcomes all their problems.

✳ LOVE STORIES IN WHICH OPPOSITES ✳ ATTRACT AND LIVE HAPPILY EVER AFTER

My Fair Lady: snobbish, intellectual man falls in love with cockney street urchin.

Sweet Home Alabama: country guy has happy romance with city girl.

Two Weeks' Notice: money-mad rich guy finds true love with non-materialistic girl.

New in Town: high-powered sun-loving Miami girl finds happiness in frozen Minnesota with small-town simple guy.

Giving all for love

 The romantic rules

The more you give to a man, the more he will love you.
The more you please a man, the more he will love you.

In fiction, the heroine is willing to give all for love. Through her selfless devotion and self-sacrifice, she wins the heart of her man. Nice story.

In the *Twilight* saga, Bella is always putting her own needs aside for others. When she goes to Forks, she is sacrificing herself for her mother's sake. She did not want to leave Phoenix, but she did, so that her mother could be happy with Phil. When Edward leaves her in *New Moon*, she is willing to sacrifice her life to get a few minutes of his voice in her head. She admires Emily, who risked losing her life and lost her looks because of her love for a werewolf. Bella is willing to give everything to Edward, who adores this selfless devotion. The message is that Bella's self-sacrificing nature makes Edward love her more and treat her more tenderly. He deeply respects her for this.

This is not the psychological reality of relationships. If someone behaves in an overly giving and self-sacrificing way, the natural tendency is to lose respect for that person. Look at the way Bella feels about Mike Newton. It is not just his physical side she finds unattractive, it is the way he is so eager to please. She sees him as being like a dog wagging its tail. She has no respect for him. Human beings tend to form pecking orders, with the dominant ones commanding respect from others and rising to the top, and the submissive ones ending up at the bottom.

Think of people you respect. They are likely to be those who don't put up with too much from others. The long-suffering martyr is likely to irritate you. When someone is willing to tolerate anything from you, you lose respect for them. The less respect you have for them, the worse you will treat them.

The message that you must sacrifice yourself in relationships is not a healthy one. If you are constantly putting your needs last, your boyfriend will lose respect for you. If you behave like a martyr, your boyfriend will treat you like one. Even decent, loving guys will find themselves taking advantage of you.

Abby loved taking care of others. She'd just qualified as a nurse, and her kind, giving nature made her fantastic at her job. She was always receiving flowers and cards from grateful patients. Abby would take extra pains to make people comfortable, anticipating their needs, always smiling, always tolerant. Her relationship with her new boyfriend went well at first. Craig was a decent enough guy, attracted to Abby's kind nature. But the problem was that she never seemed to have needs of her own. If he asked her what she'd like to do, she always said, 'I'll enjoy whatever you like.' He wasn't the tidiest of guys, and Abby patiently cleared up after him. If he needed something, she sacrificed whatever she was doing to help him. When his car broke down she left her day out shopping with her friends to come and rescue him. She lent him her car and took the bus to work, a two-hour trip. Craig hated to admit it to himself, but Abby's smiling, serene attitude started to get on his nerves. If he was irritable, she tried to soothe him. This made him more irritable with her. The more irritable he became, the more obliging she was.

In his mind, he started thinking of her as St Abigail. One evening just before bedtime Craig had been moody with

SECRET TWO: DISCOVER THE HIDDEN DANGERS OF YOUR ROMANTIC IMAGINATION

her so the next morning Abby brought him a beautifully cooked breakfast on a tray. The sight of the lovingly cooked food made something inside him snap. He told her how she made him feel and that he didn't love her any more. Abby was heartbroken. She couldn't understand what she'd done wrong.

LIONS AND LAMBS

One of the most popular lines of the *Twilight* saga is where Edward likens himself to a lion falling in love with a lamb. This is a wonderful sentence because it captures the essence of romantic stories in one powerful image. The lion's aggression is tamed by his feelings for the lamb. The lamb's gentle, self-sacrificing nature wins his love. It's poetic and romantic, but not a good basis for a real relationship. In reality, guys do not follow the rules of romantic stories. They follow the rules of human nature.

Rosalie's tragedy

If you still doubt the importance of romantic fiction in your own love life, then take another look at the *Twilight* saga. It's all in there.

Remember Rosalie's story? When Rosalie was a young girl she fell hopelessly in love with Royce King the Second, the handsome son of a wealthy man. Rosalie was so dazzled by the image of him as the Prince Charming that she didn't see who he really was. She didn't even bother to find out, because she was so in love with the fantasy. She sensed that something wasn't right, as she noticed he didn't kiss her in a very loving way. But she ignored this clue to his character and agreed to marry him. The reality of the relationship was nothing like a storybook. He and his friends raped her and left her for dead.

Rosalie had the classic Cinderella story in her head. It powerfully influenced her feelings for Royce. And it ruined her life.

BELLA'S CHARACTER

Bella is a huge fan of stories about love, like *Romeo and Juliet* and *Wuthering Heights*. She does not connect well with real human beings, but she adores romantic, fictional heroes. Throughout the *Twilight* saga she likens her own love life with Edward and Jacob to the stories she has read.

So when she meets Edward it makes perfect sense for her to fall in love with him. She is a deeply romantic girl. We find it utterly believable she would adore him. She believes the rules of romance. From reading *Wuthering Heights*, she comes to think that love redeems a man, no matter how cruel and violent. From *Romeo and Juliet*, she takes the idea that no sacrifice is too great for love. Without these beliefs, she may well have walked away from the dangerous Edward.

Throughout the books, Bella likens herself to a heroine in a love story, seeing herself as the central character in a romantic tale. So Stephenie Meyer herself recognises the power of romantic fiction in influencing people's decision-making in relationships. Bella's character is based on it.

TWILIGHT – FANTASY FOR GIRLS

Men like to look at pictures of naked fantasy women. Girls prefer love stories. Studies show that pornography can distort men's views of women. And romantic fiction can distort your ideas about guys.

It's accepted we need to be careful about pornography. Only a certain amount of sexual content can be legally shown in a film. Yet girls can be exposed to highly romantic material and no one minds. *Twilight* is a 12A. Twelve-year-olds can go and see the films, and a child of any age can read the books.

But maybe romantic films and books should be restricted, too. There should be a warning on the cover: 'Caution: This book contains explicit romantic material'.

And for films, there should be a new category. *Twilight* should be a 45H. This means it's safe for 45-year-olds to watch this film, if accompanied by their husband.

At the very least, the *Twilight* books should be accompanied with a warning:

✳ WARNING ✳

This book contains messages which may be hazardous to your love life. Please bear in mind the following:
Love will not change him.
Love will not gentle him.
A violent man is not a nice guy underneath.
Just because a man loves a woman it doesn't make up for his violent behaviour.
Love can't make an unhappy man into a happy one.
Your love can't cure him of his personal difficulties.
Love cannot make incompatible people compatible.
Love does not conquer all.
Don't give too much to a man, because he won't value you for it.
Don't try to please a man too much, he won't respect you for it.

So high-octane romances like *Twilight* can lead you into the arms of the wrong man, but for some girls, their love of *Twilight* could mean they won't end up in the arms of any man at all. Are you one of them?

CHAPTER SIX

TWILIGHT HAS RAISED THE BAR FOR MEN TOO HIGH

There's another danger if you love the *Twilight* men. Instead of rushing into a bad relationship in a romantic daze, looking at your guy with glittery, rose-tinted specs, you might do the complete opposite.

You might judge real men far too harshly because you are comparing them to Edward and Jacob. Thousands of young women are looking at the real guys around them, comparing them to the heroes of *Twilight*, and of course no human can measure up. You might feel like the girls who have joined the Facebook group 'Because of Edward Cullen, human boys have lost their charm'.

Charlotte is studying animal care at college. For the past year she has been fantasising about meeting 'her Edward'.

'I find myself sitting in classes, daydreaming. One day a newcomer arrives: Edward. In my fantasy it's the reverse of the school in Forks – I'm the student who has been there years and he's the new boy who doesn't know anybody. He notices me, but I'm the one who avoids him at first.

'Wherever I go, I like to imagine Edward following me. If I see a silver Volvo, I pretend that it's him, trying to find out where I live. When guys come up to me, I imagine him instantly appearing, consumed with jealousy, to shove them away.'

Charlotte hasn't shared her fantasies with her friends but talks about them non-stop on an online forum with fellow Twilight *fans. She knows her real-life friends are surprised she never goes out on dates.*

'There's one guy who likes me who I think of as Mike. He's just like him. He always times leaving the class so we can meet at the door and say hi. He's quite sweet, but in my head I have Edward chasing after me. I don't need a man like Mike.'

If you judge real men by comparing them to the *Twilight* heroes, then your love life is over before it starts. Obviously, compared to the fabulous Edward and Jacob, human males look second-rate. Throughout the *Twilight* series, Bella views ordinary guys on her level, like Mike, Eric and Tyler, as being inferior types of being. The thought of dating them is not in the least bit attractive to her.

Are you looking at men in the same way that Bella looks at ordinary guys? Do you see them as far beneath Edward or Jacob?

HUMAN MALES JUST AREN'T GOOD ENOUGH

If you judge guys you meet by using Edward or Jacob for a yardstick, the emotion you will feel for real guys will be contempt, and if you look at guys with contempt, you'll never fall in love. Studies show that contempt is the emotion a woman feels towards a man just before she dumps him. John Gottman, a psychologist, has analysed video footage of troubled couples talking together. He was able to predict who will break up and who will stay together. The ones who broke up were those who were showing signs of contempt. They'd started 'looking down' on their partner and seeing them as inferior.

Contempt is a basic human emotion. It is associated with the belief that another person is an inferior being, of little or no human worth. It has great destructive power. It is behind some of the worst human behaviour. In bullying, the bully feels contempt for the victim. In wars, governments spread racist propaganda about the enemy so their soldiers look down on the them. In World War Two, the American government portrayed the Japanese as a sub-human species to be eradicated like rats. When the soldier feels contempt for a set of people, that the enemy is an inferior, worthless human being, it makes it much easier to kill them. Jacob feels contempt for vampires, so he has no compunction about killing them.

The above are examples of extreme contempt, but mild contempt can affect how you relate to others. You can't love a man you see as an inferior being.

BUT MEN REALLY ARE HOPELESS!

Some of you may be thinking, OK, but real guys don't have much going for them. None of them are worth a snap of the fingers next to the *Twilight* heroes. That's just the way it is. But is it fair to compare real guys with your fantasy men?

Meet Callum, your new boyfriend:

> *Imagine you have just started seeing Callum, a guy you really like. It's not serious yet, you have just kissed a couple of times. He's nothing amazing to look at, but you like him. He's brilliant at windsurfing and makes you laugh. You like his blue eyes and strong, broad shoulders. He seems like a genuine person. You've been out with him twice and then he invites you to spend the day with him at the beach.*
>
> *You meet up, feeling a little self-conscious because you are wearing a new sparkly bikini that you're not sure*

about, so you're a bit nervous as you take off your sarong and lie down on your beach towel to sunbathe. You notice as he glances at your body.

He seems a bit distant; he doesn't look you in the eye and he's gone all quiet. He's no longer chatting and joking around. You ask him what's wrong. He doesn't answer. Ten minutes later, you're still getting the silent treatment. You ask him to be straight with you.

He sighs and takes out his mobile phone. He says, 'Look, I'll tell you the truth.' He angles the mobile phone screen so you can see and shows you a picture from a pornographic website. It is a perfect, airbrushed photo of a girl with waist-length, blonde hair extensions and huge fake breasts. Her lips are plumped with collagen and her eyelids are weighed down with false lashes. Her jawline is photoshopped into perfect symmetry and her legs are suspiciously long. She's pouting into the camera, her expression inviting, promising to fulfil every wildest fantasy. At the top of the picture you read that she's called Barbie-Lou and she loves men with big cars and big ideas.

Callum sighs, and strokes the image of Barbie-Lou with his fingertip. He says, 'The truth is, you just don't compare with Barbie-Lou here. I was really hoping I'd found someone like her. Your figure looked OK in clothes. But I look at you in your bikini now, then I look at Barbie-Lou and – to be honest – compared with her, your boobs are small and weird looking. Proper ones are huge and bouncy like Barbie-Lou's.' He points to your thighs. 'I notice there is a pocket of cellulite around here. Your stomach isn't all it could be. I'm not that impressed with your legs either. "Stumpy" is the only word to describe them. And to be honest, I don't see you offering me the kind of sex that Barbie-Lou here would. I've seen you three times and all you've offered is a bit of a snog. So it's just not going to work.'

He shows a picture of a similarly enhanced dark-haired woman. 'This is Candy. My mates rate her number one. But I'm Team Barbie-Lou. She's perfect. To be honest, because of Barbie-Lou, ordinary girls like you have lost their charm.'

How would you feel? Hurt, outraged, furious?

And rightly so. It's sick to be compared to a fantasy vision that doesn't even exist. It's not right to use a fantasy woman as a yardstick to judge you by and every cell in your body would rebel at being judged like this. It's degrading and dehumanising.

Callum is not looking at you as a human being. He has no interest in you as a person. He's seeing you as an object that can help him live out his fantasies.

And that is exactly what you're doing when you compare guys to Edward and Jacob. You're not seeing your guy as a person. You see him as an object to live out your fantasies. You wouldn't stand for it if someone did that to you. So why should you do that to him?

Looking for someone to match up to a fantasy figure is not a good basis for love. First of all, you won't find anyone. And if you do, you will not love them, only the parts of them that live up to the dream. At the end of the day, you want a guy who will love you. And how do you expect him to love you if you don't really love him?

You'd probably guess a man like Callum is never going to be happy with a real woman. And you may be right. There are concerns that guys in their mid twenties – the first generation to have been exposed to easily available porn in adolescence –

will have difficulties in forming long-term intimate relationships. Because they've learned about sexuality through pornography, they have an unreal view of how women should be.

Like guys who are fixated on fantasy images of women, if you're fixated on fantasy men then you too will struggle in relationships.

REALITY CHECK

The problem with Callum is that he believes he should try to turn his fantasy into reality. But this is never going to happen. First, the woman is not real; she's an airbrushed, posed, artificial image. Secondly, even if he met a stunning girl with an incredible body, she'd be way out of his league. Studies show that people usually end up with boyfriends or girlfriends of a similar level of attractiveness. Unless a man is rich, he will end up with a girl in his league. Ordinary men like Callum have to be satisfied with an ordinary girl. But, because in his imagination he's seen himself with a fantasy figure, part of him believes he can have this. He has enough of an ego to believe that a beautiful girl should fall for him no matter what he looks like.

In *Twilight*, Edward is way out of Bella's league; he looks like a male model or an angel. Bella is pretty, compared to the girls in a small high school like Forks, but she is not model material. She is an ordinary girl who takes no care in her appearance, wearing old sweatpants and flannel shirts. And yet Edward falls for her. Like Callum, there may be part of you that feels a beautiful man should fall for you no matter what you look like. You may be one of the girls who believe this could happen. Why shouldn't you have a guy like Edward or Jacob? (Or preferably both, like Bella.) You don't want to stick to guys in your league. They're not good enough for you. But you don't like it when an ordinary-looking guy believes he deserves a girl with film star or glamour model looks. But some *Twilight* fans are doing exactly the same thing.

If you've started feeling that you can't be satisfied with a normal-looking guy, then you've let your ego run away with you. Like Charlotte at the start of this chapter, you may be living in a make-believe world that is damaging your real love life.

IT'S NOT ALL ABOUT LOOKS THOUGH – IT'S ALL ABOUT LOVE

On the whole girls are not as shallow as guys when it comes to judging the opposite sex. Looks are not the be-all and end-all for girls. Another reason why ordinary guys seem second-rate compared to the *Twilight* heroes is they don't offer the same kind of love as Edward and Jacob, who are capable of an incredible depth of feeling. Both of them have a passionate, enduring love for Bella. Their lives are nothing without her. The driving force of their lives is to protect Bella and make her happy.

In *Twilight*, love is more intense than love in real life. The vampires love eternally, and the werewolves 'imprint'. Their love is unbreakable, all-consuming. Bella is the centre of Edward's and Jacob's existence. Their love for her defines them.

The guys around you don't offer the same thing at all. You doubt anyone could love you in the same way that Edward and Jacob love Bella. You or your friends might have experienced rather disappointing reactions from your boyfriends. They don't seem to provide a fraction of the intensity and feelings that you want.

*Emily had been seeing Charlie for some time. He played
ice hockey semi-professionally and was going on a tour of
Canada with his team, following it with a road trip across
America. He'd be away for two months. He invited Emily to
join him for part of it but she couldn't get away from work.
'I knew he'd been looking forward to the trip for a year,
but I still imagined him saying he was cancelling his road*

trip to be with me. But he didn't. He was as excited as a little boy the night before he left, while I was clinging to him, crying, which was a bit embarrassing. But I couldn't bear to be parted from him.'

She expected he would text or send her a message on Facebook the next day. But time passed without a word. When she called him, he sounded cheerful.

'I was angry he wasn't missing me more. He said he was. But he didn't act like he was. It was all him talking non-stop about his team and his travels.'

Halfway through Charlie's trip Emily had an accident.

'I wasn't looking where I was going and a car ran over my foot. I'm not saying it was the worst injury in the world, but two bones in my foot were cracked and I was in plaster and on crutches. I called him from the hospital. He was sympathetic but not all that concerned. OK, I'll admit it, I think he should have flown home early. We were in a serious relationship. I should have come first. All he did was order me some flowers and he carried on having a laugh on holiday with his mates. A true love wouldn't have done this.'

Lots of you are dissatisfied with human love. It seems like a lukewarm, unreliable thing compared to the love Bella has from Edward and Jacob. Men in real life never care for you endlessly, tell you that you are their whole existence, or marvel at your face when you are asleep. The reality of men, who seem fickle and shallow by comparison, can be like a slap in the face.

A CLOSER LOOK AT EDWARD'S FEELINGS FOR BELLA

The way that Edward loves Bella is not a normal, human love of one adult to another. It is an exaggerated version. It is a type of obsessive, all-consuming love. You might feel that this sounds very attractive. But Edward's feelings for Bella aren't like those that a man has for a woman. His love has the quality of a mother's love for her newborn child.

He not only gazes at her when she is sleeping, but he sings her a lullaby while she falls asleep in his arms. He is always picking her up and carrying her everywhere, like a small child. He attends to her physical needs, fussing about whether she is hungry, or tired. He is super-protective. He laughs indulgently at her awkward, clumsy ways. He is stern when she is misbehaving. He is obsessively protective over her, like a parent is with a tiny infant. In *Eclipse*, when he takes her to La Push to see Jacob at the werewolves' bonfire party, she feels like a child being handed over from the custody of one parent to another. Edward arranges 'babysitters' for Bella when he is away. He is highly knowledgeable and all-powerful.

You don't usually get this type of obsessive, parental love from men. And if you did, you'd get fed up with it after a while. Bella herself finds it smothering. She longs to be a vampire too, not just to be with Edward forever, but to be an equal to him.

LOVE IS MORE IMPORTANT THAN LIFE ITSELF

Another reason that *Twilight* is appealing is that Edward and Jacob feel that their love for Bella is more important than life itself. They would lay down their lives for her. You might look at the men around you and feel cheated. Most guys wouldn't prefer to die than be without you.

Emily broke up with Charlie shortly after he returned from his ice hockey tour and road trip.

'He'd proved to me that he wasn't too bothered about being with me for a lifetime. I was only part of his life,

and that's not enough for true love. He wouldn't even sacrifice his dream holiday when I was injured, so he'd hardly sacrifice his life for me.'

Emily is now single and looking for the man who will put her at the centre of his life.

In the *Twilight* saga, love between a man and a woman is glorified as a divine, heady state of being that is so precious that it is more important than anything else in the world. No sacrifice is too great. Death is preferable to losing love.

This makes great, heart-wrenching fiction. Like many romantic stories, *Twilight* gives the message that love is more important than life itself. When Edward goes to Italy to provoke the Volturi, because he can't face an existence without Bella in it, you sigh and think, how romantic.

It all makes real-life relationships look drab in comparison. How many of the guys you see around you would die to save their girlfriends? Most men don't see love as being more important than life itself. They see football as being more important than life itself.

So it is disappointing when you look around at human males. Love is not a life and death matter for them. You are not likely to get a guy who would sacrifice his life for you. You count yourself lucky if he sacrifices a night out with the boys for you.

After *Twilight*, you dream of experiencing a love which is more important than life or death. This dream is a reality for some people. Do you want a man who values your love more than life itself? The good (or rather bad) news is you can. Thousands of young people kill themselves after a relationship break up because they can't face life without their loved one.

✦ AN ALL-CONSUMING LOVE ✦

Mark Speight was a popular TV presenter who was inseparable from his fiancée, Natasha Collins. She had been an up-and-coming actress until she was severely injured in a road accident that left her in a coma. He cared for her, helping her recover. In January 2008 she died of a drugs overdose.

Mark was devastated and unable to come to terms with the tragedy. His family, and Natasha's mother, tried desperately to support him, yet he was convinced his future was one of nothing but empty loneliness. He spoke about how he couldn't contemplate life without her. Three months after her death he left a note for Natasha's mother and disappeared. He was missing for six days before his body was discovered hanging in an empty building.

Within a few months his family and Natasha's gathered for a third funeral. Mark's mother had died; her health had been ruined by grief.

His father now grieves alone. He maintains a shrine of Mark's childhood toys, posters and photos. He says, 'It's somewhere I can feel close to him.'

The reality of 'love for you is more important than life' is desperately sad. It's not romantic in the slightest. It's only appealing and dramatic in fiction.

Imagine a male in your life you care about – your brother or a relative or a friend. Imagine he goes out with a girlfriend that he falls deeply in love with but she dies suddenly from some rare undiagnosed heart condition.

Would you want him to die rather than live without her? Would you want to find your brother dead with an empty bottle of pills in his hand, or find a friend lying with slashed wrists? Could you bear to read a suicide note that says 'I couldn't live without her'?

Of course not. You would want your brother or friend to live. There are many things worth living for apart from romantic love.

> ## ✳ A DISTURBING FACT ✳
>
> Some cultures believe love is more important than life or death. In some parts of the world people believe a girl should not want to live as a widow if she truly loved her man.
>
> In India, 18-year-old Roop Kanwar was married for just eight months when her husband died. At her husband's funeral, her relatives covered her in cooking oil and she was burned alive on her husband's funeral pyre. She was idolised as a saint for having made such a sacrifice.
>
> This tradition of widows burning themselves alive at their husband's funeral – called *sati* – is illegal, but still happens today.

The message in *Twilight* is that obsessive, dangerous love is somehow wonderful, that Bella would be better off dead than without Edward and vice versa.

This idea belongs firmly in the realm of fiction. The reality is that you don't want to experience this kind of love.

Men and women do not make each other the centre of their existence. Life is about more – much more – than romantic love alone. Human love at its best does not demand barbaric sacrifices. It is not so consuming that it destroys lives. It works because two people give to each other equally. Healthy love is when you value your own happiness and well-being, *and* you value your partner's. You can love a person deeply, but know that if you lost them, it would be devastating, but one day your heart would heal.

Do not expect your boyfriend to love at all costs. A normal, happy type of love is not unbreakable. It is not all-consuming.

Most guys will not consider love more important than life itself.
And a good thing, too.

SECRET TWO: SUMMARY

The *Twilight* story may be hazardous to your love life if it
influences you in these ways:

- You think your love can cure a dangerous man.
- You believe an unhappy man can make you happy.
- You believe an incompatible man could be your
  soulmate.
- You think your love can change him into the man you
  want him to be.
- You become fixated on a fantasy image of men, instead
  of relating to real men.
- You become fixated on a fantasy version of love,
  instead of real love.

So what can you about it? Let's take a closer look at your
feelings for the *Twilight* heroes.

* **SECRET THREE** *

Loving a Human

(Only a real man can fulfil your needs as a woman!)

CHAPTER 7

YOU NEED A REAL MAN IN YOUR LIFE, NOT A GOD IN HUMAN FORM

Have you been in love with a guy? Ever worshipped one?

There's a difference.

When you read *Twilight*, you have strong emotional reactions to Edward or Jacob. They trigger intense feelings; it feels like love. They have amazing super-human qualities. They are way above you in their powers, their looks, everything; and you have them on a high pedestal. They are totally superior to you and every other human being.

That isn't love, it's worship – the way you would feel about a god. It is definitely a strong emotion. But it's not the same kind of love that one human being gives to another.

The word 'worship' originally meant to acknowledge someone's worthiness, but it came to be more about kneeling in subservient submission. And that's the problem. Seeing someone as being worthy of worship means putting yourself below them. That isn't adult human love, because in adult love you are both equals.

Edward and Jacob are like earthbound deities, rather than normal guys on your level. If they lost their incredible looks and powers, your feelings for them would change.

When you're looking for a guy who can measure up to Edward or Jacob, you're looking for someone you can worship. And the trouble is, if you found someone to worship, the balance between you would be all wrong.

Bella recognises this. She says she can't see her relationship with Edward working if she has to carry on playing the part of Lois Lane to Edward's Superman. This is one of the reasons she wants him to change her. She tells him they need to be equals. She knows the balance of their relationship is unhealthy.

A relationship in which one person worships the other as superior is not a path to happiness.

Tanya met Luke in her first year at college. She was studying to be a physiotherapist and Luke was at a top acting school.

'*I met him at a party and couldn't believe he was interested in me. He had chiselled looks and beautiful clothes. I'd always thought I was ordinary-looking and was amazed he was attracted to me. And he was truly a talented person, destined for success.*'

Tanya adored Luke and was proud to show him off to her friends.

'*He had a natural style and magnetism that made him the centre of attention at any party. All my friends used to jokingly refer to him as "the god"!*'

But they didn't have much in common. He was from a wealthy, arty background, and she felt completely out of place when she went with him to his parents' holiday villa in Italy. She found it hard to admit that despite the dream surroundings, she didn't enjoy herself one bit.

'*They kept using words like "postmodern" and "contemporaneous". Half the time I felt I needed a dictionary. One night they threw a sumptuous dinner party and asked me to quote my favourite lines from Shakespeare! As if I had any. I had to learn to like fancy food like truffles and chanterelle mushrooms. I prefer the simpler things in life, myself.*'

Tanya put Luke first in every decision she made. Her spare time became taken up with grooming herself and finding fashionable clothes to keep up with him. She never bothered him with any of her problems, as he'd once said he had an ex-girlfriend who was an emotional leech, who'd needed propping up all the time.

She found herself doing everything within her power to please him. 'I spent my spare time accompanying him to student plays which, to be frank, were boring. He tended to overspend the allowance he got from his parents so I lent him money. Most times he forgot to pay me back.'

About six months into their relationship Tanya went to an all-night party with Luke and his trendy friends. She was exhausted the next day as she'd had to listen to them discussing Ibsen, a boring playwright she couldn't care less about. But she'd forced herself out to the shops to find a new outfit for yet another night watching a play. At the clothes shop she suddenly burst into tears.

'I'd never felt anxiety like that before. It hit me from nowhere. I realised I didn't have a penny left in my bank account and the thought of going out again that night terrified me. A shop assistant made me a cup of tea and I found myself clinging to her arm. I was overwhelmed with loneliness, which frightened me because I couldn't possibly be lonely as I had a boyfriend. That day was the start of long months of me struggling to be happy again.'

Tanya was lonely with Luke as he didn't really know her, only the person she pretended to be. She realised that their relationship was a problem. Tanya truly worshipped Luke. But their relationship wasn't making her happy.

'I told Luke the way I felt. He accused me of being like his "needy" ex. He complained that every woman he went *out with tried to suck the life out of him. I was the one in misery but he was the one complaining.'*

After a lot of pain, Tanya decided that she'd never feel good enough for him and he'd never be able to give her what she needed. She finally made the decision to break it off.

'I spent three months in despair at the break-up. One night my friends persuaded me to go to a nightclub and there he was, Luke, out with a new girlfriend. And it's funny – usually it's supposed to be a massive trauma when you see your ex with a new girlfriend. But for me it was a sudden moment of insight. She was another average-looking girl, similar to me, and she was looking at him with adoration in her eyes. And I realised – that was exactly what he was into. Luke loved to have a girlfriend who wasn't a threat to him and who did whatever he said. He was basking in her worship and she was basking in his reflected glory. And for the first time I was happy to be out of that relationship.'

The problem with worshipping a man as a god is simple: it isn't emotionally fulfilling. It won't meet your human needs. Only another human, an equal, can truly understand you.

Sharing the experience of being human with all the difficulties, joys and vulnerabilities that go with it is one of the reasons men and women want to form a close relationship with each other. You need a partner with whom you share enough in common to be able to do this. If he either is, or believes himself to be, far above you, he will not be able to empathise with you.

You don't need your man to be like a god. If you want a god in your life, then you can turn to religion. You could practise the faith you were born into, or explore some new spiritual possibilities.

God belongs in heaven, not on your arm.

After Tanya recovered from her break-up with Luke, she was cautious about men for a long time. But when she met Paul, she felt instantly comfortable with him. He was from a similar background to herself and liked down-to-earth pleasures, like eating fish and chips at the seaside or staying in with a huge bowl of popcorn to watch the latest Hollywood blockbuster. He didn't have chiselled looks, but was attractive enough in an ordinary way.

'It took me some time to get used to being in an equal relationship. Sometimes I missed the status of having a guy like Luke at my side and I acted as if I was subservient to Paul. He laughed at me for trying to put him first! He only ever wanted to be on an equal basis to me and I soon learned to enjoy connecting with him. I felt good about myself in his company. And I was being myself, which made me feel much closer to him.'

When she fell in love with him, it was the love of one human being to another, not the hero worship she'd felt for Luke. It was a much happier place to be.

YOU DON'T NEED THE PERFECT GUY

A problem with *Twilight* is that it has given you a vision of perfection when it comes to guys. You are falling into the trap of thinking perfection will make you happy. But it won't. The perfection trap is one of the main causes of unhappiness in modern life.

In today's society, you're told to look for happiness through striving to be the best. At school and in your job, you're told to work as hard as you can, and that if you can only improve yourself and your life then you will be happy.

There is a huge industry geared to helping you improve your mind, your body, your abs, your emotions, your kitchen, your bathroom, your hair. You just have to open a magazine or switch on the TV to be bombarded with adverts saying you should be slimmer, richer, more successful at work, have shinier hair and nicer eyelashes. You are told that if you play your cards right you can get the perfect skin and a better-shaped bottom. If you choose the right tampon, you can be confident and happier.

TV programmes and films show a fantasy version of life. Hollywood produces film after film about gorgeous people who live in huge, perfect houses. Magazines are full of the rich and famous. Images of people like Paris Hilton, Victoria Beckham, Cheryl Cole and so on are plastered everywhere, next to adverts and articles showing you how to be more like them. The philosophy is that more is better.

So does all this striving for a perfect life make you happy?

No, it doesn't.

Studies of happiness show that even though our lives are getting better and better and it is in our power to improve ourselves to near perfection, it is not making us one bit happier. Beautiful people are no happier than plain ones. Once you are out of poverty, getting richer and richer will not make you happier. Psychological research shows that if someone gets something good, like a lottery win, they'll feel pleased for a while, but that boost will steadily fade until they return to the level of happiness they were experiencing before.

More is not better.

Those good-looking, super-rich personalities are no happier than the average person. People with seemingly perfect lives are just as susceptible to divorce, depression and alcoholism as the rest of us.

Why doesn't more make you happier? Because you keep adjusting your expectations so that they're higher and higher. When you buy your first home, you may be very happy in a tiny one-bedroom flat. Soon, you realise how much better it would be to have a spare room for guests – and a garden. The girl next door has an outside jacuzzi in hers... So you feel dissatisfied and want more. Your hair is much shinier with your new conditioner, but it's still nothing like Jennifer Aniston's.

Human beings always compare themselves with people who have more. And modern life has a way of making you feel that who you are as a person and what you have in life isn't good enough. This causes a huge amount of restlessness and dissatisfaction, despite the fact that many people today are safer, better fed and richer than at any other time in history.

Comparing yourself to people better off than you and wanting more will make you unhappy and dissatisfied. Happiness does not come from perfection, because perfection can never be achieved. As soon as you achieve your goal, you set the bar higher.

✶ NONE OF THESE WILL MAKE YOU ✶ FUNDAMENTALLY HAPPIER:

Toned abs
Shinier hair
A million pounds
Losing half a stone
Getting a promotion
An expensive car

Comparing the men around you to Edward and Jacob is falling into the same trap; the trap of thinking that perfection is what you need, and anything second best cannot make you happy. Applying the 'more is better' thinking to our guys is the same mistake we are making in the rest of our lives. The two perfect guys, Edward and

Jacob, have been created, and you crave that kind of perfection from your man. But a perfect guy won't make you any happier than a decent guy. Having an ordinary human guy to love and love you back is already a wonderful thing.

A DREAM OF HEAVEN

It's human nature to hope and strive for a wonderful future. But in ancient times, people didn't expect a better future during their lifetimes. With disease, hunger and death surrounding them every day, they didn't look for happiness on earth. Instead, they imagined a better future in the afterlife. And the way to get there was to be a good person, avoid sin and please the gods.

Times have changed and nowadays, you expect to be happy. And the way to get there is by making yourself and your life better. The sins you want to avoid are the sins of being too ugly, too fat, too poor, or failing. You are told that by living right, eating the right foods, doing the right exercise, getting more money, looking after your skin and finding the right guy you can stay young and beautiful, be loved forever, be wonderfully happy and cheat death.

Twilight is the perfect story for today. You hope to find heaven on earth. *Twilight* shows you a young woman who achieves it. She lives with the god-like Edward for eternity, perfectly beautiful, never ageing, free from human weakness and disease.

It is the twenty-first-century dream.

LOVE AND WELL-BEING

Love won't make you immortal or stop you from ageing, but there is plenty of evidence to show that being in a steady, loving relationship will give you emotional and even health benefits. These benefits are over and above the financial advantages that couples enjoy.

Having a loving, supportive partner can help protect you from the effects of stress. This was shown in a scientific study of people's stress reactions to a mild electric shock. One study looked at the stress responses of women to a mild electric shock. The stress response was much lower for women holding their husband's hand, compared to women holding a stranger's hand.

Good emotional support from a man can help buffer you against the difficulties in life. Being in a steady, loving relationship seems to give some protection from becoming depressed. Happily married women have lower rates of depression compared to unhappily married, single or divorced women. And people in good relationships report greater life satisfaction. Women in happy relationships also have a strong immune response. Those who are happily married live on average four years longer.

But research reveals that you won't benefit from just any relationship. One study suggested that being in a stressful marriage was as bad for your heart as smoking. A loveless marriage was as strong a predictive factor for heart disease as being a smoker.

Research also suggests that women appear to be particularly vulnerable to the affects of a bad marriage. Work stress didn't put them at higher risk of heart attacks, whereas marital stress did. Another study has found that physical wounds take longer to heal in couples showing hostility to each other.

If you have left a bad relationship, but are far from 'over' him, your health may still suffer. Research shows that women happily out of a bad relationship have a better immune response than those still hung up on their ex.

THE LURE OF THE FAMILIAR

Psychology research shows that we are attracted to what is familiar. This is why companies spend millions of pounds advertising their brands, so that you see images of the same product on billboards,

TV adverts and magazines. If you see a familiar brand in the supermarket, you are much more likely to buy it. So if the brand of man you know is terrible, you will gravitate towards a similar type. If you know men as cruel, unfaithful, controlling, selfish, you'll be drawn towards that kind.

If you believe that men are inevitably selfish, boorish, unfaithful, bad tempered, it is likely to become a self-fulfilling prophecy. Having this view of men will mean you won't look very hard for a good one. You'll go out with a guy, see he has many faults, and just accept that this is the way it is; that your suspicions are confirmed and men are no good. You will settle for your image of how men are. And then when he treats you badly, and dumps you, broken-hearted, you can say to everyone: 'I told you so, they are all worthless.' Research shows that having an optimistic, positive attitude will make you more likely to have good experiences. And this applies to your attitudes to men.

So how do you change?

You need to develop a balanced view of men that recognises that while some of them are dangerous, there are plenty of good men and some of them are absolutely wonderful. You need to build a positive view of men, as well as a realistic understanding that some men are not good news and worth avoiding.

But how do you build a positive view of men when your only experience of them is just how awful they can be?

CHAPTER 8

WONDERFUL, WONDERFUL MEN

OK, so they're not all wonderful.

It's a reality that men perpetrate many of the horrors in this world. Men are typically responsible for many of the worst acts and events in history, from the massacres of Ghenghis Khan to the terrorism of Osama bin Laden. And a minority of men treat their women abominably.

But they are also responsible for some of the most wonderful things in the world. There are billions of men on the planet so there's a good chance many of them will be decent guys, and some of them will be amazing.

Half of all marriages last forever and many of them are happy. Some couples, the 'swans' I talked about earlier, stay madly in love with each other their whole lives. And millions of women have a decent, loving man with whom they contentedly spend their lives.

If you think real men are inferior to the *Twilight* heroes, then your mind will look for evidence to support your belief. This is the way your brain works. Research shows your mind will go looking for facts that fit in with what you already believe. This is why it's very difficult to change someone's mind. When you have arguments with friends or family, how easy is it to persuade them that you're right? It's human nature to try to cling onto beliefs.

So if you're of the opinion that real guys are no good compared to Edward or Jacob, you'll look around you and pick out all the reasons to confirm that it's true. You can't help it. It happens unconsciously. Once you have a belief, your mind will filter out all the stuff that goes against it and seize on the stuff which supports it.

Sixteen-year-old Shannon was reading the Twilight *saga for the fifth time. She was firmly Team Edward and, with her mind full of visions of Edward's diamond skin and flawless bone structure, she reluctantly put* Breaking Dawn *down to get ready for her date with Alex.*

Alex drove her to the local theme park. He was fit and tanned from his summer working outside on a farm. She found out he was sporty, like her, and they both loved running. She had a fantastic day with him going on all the white-knuckle rides and cheesy fairground stalls and eating junk food. She liked the way Alex put his arm round her protectively on the roller coaster.

However, her brain registered the following facts:

He didn't drive a sleek silver Volvo, he drove an old Ford.
He didn't have diamond skin; instead, he had a small spot on his chin.
He screamed when he was on the Death Plunge.
His breath didn't smell of a heady perfume, it smelled of burgers and onions.
He didn't tell her she was his whole existence.

She couldn't help picking out the ways he wasn't as good as Edward. So she didn't feel very elated after the date. When her best friend asked her how the date went, she said it was OK, nothing special.

In reality Alex was a great guy, well suited to Shannon. But, convinced no human was good enough, she couldn't see it.

So how do you change this?

You have to do the opposite of picking out all the negatives in men. You need to look for proof that real guys can be great.

THE FANTASTIC THINGS ABOUT REAL MEN

Men at their best are amazing; much more heroic than Edward or Jacob. Don't believe me? Read on...

Real men are brave

Psychology research shows men are far more willing to take risks than women. Men are generally the more courageous sex.

There are a lot of incredibly brave real men in the world. You don't need to fantasise about it – plenty of men have died for you already, and continue to do so today.

For a start, have a look at a war memorial near you, full of young men who died in World Wars One and Two. They fought to protect their country so future generations could be free.

Every day, you do something because men were willing to risk their lives for you to do it. Have you crossed a large bridge lately? Have you admired a cathedral? The death rate for men working on huge construction projects was astronomical in the past and even in modern times workers die. The construction of the Channel Tunnel claimed ten lives, while four people died repairing a bridge on the M5 motorway. Women will rarely risk their lives like this.

How about your food? Do you enjoy eating fish and seafood? Every year on average 30 trawlermen die in British seas. Think of that next time you eat a plate of fish fingers.

Farming has the highest death rate of any occupation, due to the dangers of working with large machinery. In 2009, 38 farm workers lost their lives in the UK – all but one were male. So you could say even the bowl of cereal you have in the morning has a price tag of a risked life attached to it. The film *Blood Diamond* exposes the brutality and death involved in the diamond trade. But men die all the time to get food like wheat and fish to us. You could write a film called *Blood Corn Flakes* or *Blood Prawns*. (It might not be the same hit at the box office though.)

It is considered acceptable for a man to risk his life in the course of his work within certain industries. It's so normal that you don't even think about it. Of course, some women have dangerous occupations, too, but the statistics are clear: the highest death rates are for mining, farming, forestry, fishing and construction, all jobs where men far outnumber women.

But it's not just indirectly that men sacrifice their lives for others. Men are far more likely to voluntarily put their lives on the line to save others; for example, by working as firemen, or mountain and sea rescuers.

In modern life, you're encouraged to believe that risk-taking is wrong. Safety first is the current mantra. Yet risk-taking is a vital part of life; nothing worthwhile was ever achieved without taking risks.

Real men are inspirational

There are men with huge hearts who've changed the world with their love of humanity, such as Gandhi, the Dalai Lama, Martin Luther King and William Wilberforce.

There are inspirational men in the most unexpected places. Oskar Schindler was a German industrialist who profited from the misery of World War Two to become a multi-millionaire. Yet he spent everything to save thousands of Jewish men, women and children from the gas chambers. He died penniless.

Men's urge to love is just as strong as ours. Another inspirational man, Dave Pelzer, demonstrates this. As a little boy, Dave Pelzer was beaten, starved and tortured by his mother. He writes about his experiences in his book *A Child Called 'It'*. Yet this treatment did not destroy his capacity to love. With great courage, he rose above these terrible experiences and went on to be a loving husband and father.

Real men are powerful

If you like the idea of power and danger (and you really shouldn't – you really don't want a dangerous guy!) then the male of our species ticks the box. There's no other creature more dangerous and aggressive than the human male. Most other animals avoid a fight if they can. But human males destroy and kill like no other species on the planet. They are capable of incredible violence. Men are far more likely than women to murder or physically attack other people.

Compared to the human male, you are a lamb; compared to you, the average guy is as strong as a lion. His upper body strength is 50 per cent more powerful than yours. He has more red blood cells and a bigger chest, so has more cardiovascular capability than you. He has more muscle than you. He has less body fat than you. He is, on average, at least half a foot taller than you. He can run faster, jump higher and lift more than you. He is much stronger than you, and could easily overpower you and kill you with his bare hands.

But nearly all men choose not to use their power. They have the capacity but are self-controlled. Most men desire and adore women, the physically weaker sex.

Your average guy is like a lion that chooses to live like a lamb.

The technological achievements of real men

Men typically have more interest in technology than women. Men invented the telephone, the television, space travel, aeroplanes, computers and the Internet. Men discovered penicillin, anaesthetic and the contraceptive pill. They figured out how to build bridges, roads and railways. All of these things make your life easier and richer, and give you a quality of life that earlier generations only dreamed about.

Men are the ones doing most of the great technological and scientific work. It is mostly men, not women, who are working away in the vital areas of engineering, computer science, maths, physics and chemistry.

Are men naturally better at this type of work? The jury is out whether men have more technological ability than women. Some scientists believe that females are naturally more talented at communication and social skills, and males at understanding systems. Men do seem to be able to visualise things in their heads better than girls.

But these differences in ability are small, if indeed they exist at all. The more obvious difference between men and women is not ability, but inclination. Despite years of greater equality of access to education, most women are still not interested in becoming engineers or physicists. Most women are not entranced by the workings of the internal combustion engine. While men talk excitedly about a new design of carburettor, women typically roll their eyes and yawn.

Whether this difference in our interest in technology is due to nature, nurture or lack of encouragement, men can take the credit for most of today's greatest technological miracles.

Real men are funny

Studies have shown that men are more likely than women to show off their sense of humour, to crack jokes and make others laugh. Some scientists believe this is because of aggression levels. Most jokes and funny comments have a target, and so are a mild form of hostility. Men tend to be more aggressive than women, and hence make more jokes.

Whatever the theory behind it, the world is full of funny men that help make life worth living. And funny is sexy: women find comedians attractive whatever their looks, from men like Russell Brand and David Walliams to Ricky Gervais and Johnny Vegas.

UNTOLD STORIES

There are lots of good men you will never hear about. These are not men who would have a movie made about them or be held up as examples in history classes. They live quietly and unheralded, and leave the world unremembered except by their families and friends. Yet the stories of these men are often ones of kindness, integrity, hard work, devoted parenting and dedication.

Millions of men have just such a story: fathers who come home from work and then spend their evening caring for their family; husbands who support their wives through illness and disability; men who work two jobs to try to give their children a better life; men who give their free time to a cause they believe in, making a small part of the world a better place.

All men and women have their strengths and faults and few can be described as perfect, but millions of men deserve, in their last days, to look back on their lives and feel proud of the way that they have lived. Most women aren't looking for a hero, but a decent man who they can respect, and one that respects them.

Maybe you have such a man in your family? A great-grandfather who arrived home from World War Two to a low paid, hard job and spent the rest of his life supporting his wife and bringing up his family. Or a father who gives his free time to you and your siblings, doing what he can for your happiness.

These untold stories don't make great novels – we prefer the drama of the *Twilight* heroes. But nonetheless they are ordinary heroes, men who deserve our respect.

EDWARD AND JACOB – ARE THEY SO GREAT?

Are Edward or Jacob inspirational compared to real-life men?

Ordinary men have used their lives to contribute to the happiness of others. Edward and Jacob could do an immense amount of good. Think how many lives Edward and Jacob could save with their incredible strength and powers. Perhaps we shouldn't judge others by their abilities; rather, we should judge them by what they choose to *do* with their abilities.

Edward and Jacob could be superheroes, saving people and tracking down villains. Yet all they do each day is fuss around Bella, mooch about and tinkle on the piano (Edward) or mess about with campfires (Jacob). They are immortal; it's not as if they don't have the time. At the very least, Edward could do something useful with all his money. It wouldn't take him any effort to help the starving, but he chooses to spend his money on designer clothes and expensive cars. When Edward witnesses the people being massacred by the Volturi in *New Moon*, he just stands by, shrugs it off and gets back to his usual obsessing over Bella.

When you compare all the achievements of real-life men with Edward and Jacob, then Edward and Jacob do not really look so amazing. Edward's main achievement in life was in overcoming his urge to suck the blood out of human beings. Jacob's was in not ripping people into shreds if he got into a temper.

Real men are far more inspirational, noble and brave than this.

YOUR IDEAL REAL MAN

To find a great boyfriend it's a good idea to have a positive image of the type of man you need. The *Twilight* heroes are not a good basis for this, because they are impossibly perfect and dangerous at the same time.

✳ EXERCISE ✳

Think of some real men you like and admire. They could be men you know personally. If not, then use real-life examples you have learned about from books, TV, the news or films.

Think about the qualities you love in your favourite men. Don't include looks, as it goes without saying you want a guy to be physically attractive. You need a positive image of a man that goes under the surface. Good looks alone won't make you happy.

Now list all of those qualities you like in the men that you admire.

What do the lists have in common? Does one attribute come up time and time again? Or is one particular quality more important than all the others?

These are the kind of qualities you should be looking for in your real man.

If you build up a positive image of the man you want, you're more likely to spot him. It's easier to find something if you know what you are looking for. And you're more likely to persevere until you find him.

Here's how one girl changed her view of men:

> Suzi had been hurt in her last relationship. Cam was a lively, fun guy, with a great sense of humour, always the one making everyone crack up with laughter. He worked in sales and his personality made him great at his job. People warmed to him easily.
>
> Suzi had some great times with him, but as their

relationship developed, the problems emerged. Cam liked to make a joke, but no one could escape being a target of his humour, including Suzi herself. He used to make fun of her appearance. He said in front of his friends one day that her new green dress 'made her look like Shrek, but not in a good way'. Suzi was hurt and Cam got annoyed, accusing her of having no sense of humour.

About six months into the relationship, Suzi's aunt died in a car crash after falling asleep at the wheel, and Suzi was heartbroken. She was very close to her aunt, who'd been like a second mother to her.

Unfortunately, Cam couldn't take her sadness seriously. He didn't seem to grasp why Suzi was so upset. He'd lost a relative some time ago, and he hadn't really been affected.

Things came to a head at her aunt's funeral. Suzi heard him cracking a joke, outside in the graveyard. She heard him say, 'I want to die peacefully in my sleep like Suzi's aunt. Not screaming in fear like the passengers in her car.' Suzi burst into tears, there was a huge scene, and they broke up.

Afterwards, Suzi felt pessimistic about men. She hadn't had a great relationship with her father. Like Cam, he was not a sensitive man and rode roughshod over other people's feelings.

After she finished with Cam, she began to believe that the right guy didn't exist. She was a Twilight fan and just couldn't see how any real guy could have Edward's selfless devotion, or Jacob's all-enveloping warmth.

Suzi needed to develop a positive image of a man for her future, so this is what she did. The real-life men she most liked were Monty Roberts, the horse whisperer, and her cousin Richard. She thought about why she liked them so much.

Suzi had been inspired by Monty Roberts from reading about his life in his book, The Man Who Listens to Horses. *Monty Roberts, a horse trainer from California, is famous for discovering a way of working with horses that uses kindness, not cruelty. Monty has a deep understanding of the horse's mind and has discovered how to communicate with them using body language.*

This was her list of qualities she loved in her two favourite men:

<u>Monty</u>	<u>Richard</u>
Determined	*Kind*
Loves animals	*Loves animals*
Understanding	*Clever*
Kind	*Funny*
Knowledgeable	*Honest and genuine*
Clever	*Understanding*
Brave	*Knows me well*
Honest and genuine	*Listens to me*

Suzi thought about what the two guys she most admired had in common. They both loved animals and they were both honest and genuine guys. But she realised that the most important thing that they shared was their understanding and kindness.

She realised this was what was missing from Cam. He had some great qualities, but he lacked empathy.

Suzi was a sensitive girl who felt things very deeply. She realised that her ideal man would need to be a very understanding type of person. Her dream man would need to be aware of her feelings, and be kind enough to be careful with them.

The brand of man she knew so far was cruel with his words – she needed to find a new sort of guy. So she built up a positive image of the kind of person she was looking for – a man who possessed the qualities of empathy, sensitivity and kindness.

When she started dating again, she was able to quickly recognise signs that a guy wasn't kind.

Then she met Joe at a friend's house. Joe had just returned home after a year out doing volunteer work at a school in Malaysia. From the way he talked about working with the children, she could tell he was kind. When he asked her to go out with him she said yes. They have been happily together ever since.

So having a positive yet balanced view of men won't make you more vulnerable to being hurt – it may make you less vulnerable.

Of course there are still risks in relationships. When you fall for someone, you risk being hurt. You expose yourself to the possibility of rejection.

You may have been hurt so are thinking that someone like Edward or Jacob is what you need – someone who loves you so deeply he would never hurt you.

But even Bella was not immune. Edward ended his relationship with Bella in *New Moon*, causing Bella incredible hurt which never fully healed while she was human. Jacob's feelings for Bella changed when he imprinted on Renesmee. Falling in love with a guy leaves you vulnerable, but you can minimise risk by making emotionally intelligent relationship choices. Just because it hasn't happened so far doesn't mean that there is no human male out there who is capable of making you happy. There are ways to improve your ability to choose well. Lots of women have made good choices and are enjoying the benefits of a loving relationship.

SECRET THREE: SUMMARY

The secret of loving a human is:

- Loving a man as an equal.
- Judging a man for himself, not how he measures up to a fantasy image.
- Looking for a person, not perfection.
- Liking men and having positive expectations of them.

How do you pick the right one for you?

SECRET FOUR

Knowing Yourself

(What you can learn from Bella)

CHAPTER 9

HOW WELL DO YOU KNOW YOURSELF?

Why is it that some girls seem to meet the right guy and others just have a string of unhappy relationships?

Is it just a matter of bad luck? Sometimes...

But often, it's bad judgment.

Some girls go from one unsuitable man to another because they haven't a clue who they are as a person and what they need in their man.

WHO ARE YOU? ARE YOU SELF-AWARE?

Most people say yes when asked these questions. But as a human being, you only have a limited sense of self-awareness. You don't fully know what kind of person you are, what would make you happy or how others see you.

Psychology research shows we are unable to see ourselves accurately or know what we really want. You may *think* you know what makes you happy or unhappy. After all, you are the only person who has access to your inner thoughts and feelings. You are the only person who really knows what it is like to be you.

But for most people life is a process of discovering the difference between what you think you want and the reality. This is why people are always changing their minds. How many times have you thought something would be great and it turned out it wasn't? Or the other way around?

Five common ways we are blind to ourselves

1) We don't know for sure what makes us unhappy

How happy do you think you'd be after the following: ending up in a wheelchair, seeing a loved one die, being diagnosed with cancer? Most people think traumatic and distressing life events like this permanently affect your level of happiness.

Yet research shows that, in time, most people recover from these experiences to be just as happy as before. And some people even believe their lives have been enhanced by these terrible experiences. They say they have learned to appreciate life more. So even if you were permanently disabled, you'd probably be as happy as before in time.

Why does this seem wrong? Because you are predicting how you would feel by the way you feel now. The thought of being in a wheelchair fills you with horror, so you assume that's how it will be. But in reality, if it did happen in the future you'd feel differently.

2) We don't know for sure what makes us happy

How happy will you be when you finally land that dream job? Do you see yourself in Jimmy Choos, banking a lovely fat salary and booking yourself a holiday to Hawaii? Looks great, doesn't it?

The reality, however, is that you'll probably return to the same level of happiness as you have now. Studies show that when we dream of the future, we don't put much detail in the vision. We just have a few fuzzy, positive images. This is why it looks so good. The dream doesn't show the detail of the future. It doesn't show the punishing commute to your dream job, the blisters from your Jimmy Choos, the cranky boss, the boorish client with bad breath and wandering hands.

3) We have a rosy view of ourselves

Many people aren't particularly attractive or pleasant. Yet studies show nearly everyone thinks of themselves as being sensitive, popular, honest, attractive, friendly and warm. We have a flattering view of ourselves.

When asked to rate themselves and others in questionnaires, people generally rate themselves higher on positive personality traits than other people rate them. And those who have the rosiest view of themselves are actually rated by others as having negative traits, such as hostility and irritability. People generally see themselves as being more popular than they are.

4) We're unaware of our own incompetence

Time after time psychology research has shown that people have an overly positive idea of their abilities. Whether it's sense of humour, driving skills or playing tennis, people fail to recognise their own incompetence.

Think you are a better-than-average driver? So does most of the rest of the population! We can't all be better-than-average drivers. People see themselves as being much more talented than they are. This trait is behind the success of shows like *The X Factor* and *Britain's Got Talent* – we love the initial auditions where self-deluded individuals caterwaul, caper and blunder their way to public humiliation. Without this common blind spot, these shows wouldn't exist. If only the truly talented turned up to audition, they would be short and comparatively dull shows.

5) Other people are better than you at predicting how you will feel

This sounds absurd. You are the best judge of how you feel about things, right? After all, you are the only person who knows how you feel inside. But studies show people are very poor at predicting how they'll feel in a given situation.

Here's an example. You are asked to predict how much you'll enjoy a speed date with a certain man, let's call him Fred. What would you rather do? Read Fred's profile, look at his photo and judge for yourself? Or have information on how much another girl enjoyed a speed date with Fred last week? Which method will be more accurate in predicting your enjoyment? If you use the other girl's opinion, your prediction will be far more accurate. Someone who has been there and done it is in a much better position to tell you how you'll feel. But no one believes this. Humans like to judge for themselves. They cling to the idea that their viewpoint is unique.

IF YOU DON'T KNOW YOURSELF...

Let's take this understanding that we lack self-awareness into the world of relationships.

It's not easy to predict what kind of person will make you happy. If you don't know, is it any surprise you'll be stumbling in the dark? You can't choose well if you don't have an accurate picture of your own personality. Lack of self-awareness can lead you to pick the wrong man.

Ever seen a friend do this? Have you realised immediately the man is not going to make her happy and the relationship is heading towards the rocks? It's usually easier to spot when other people do it.

 Nineteen-year-old Tina was attracted to the strong, silent type. She thought men like this were manly. Tina, in contrast, was a very sociable girl.

'I fell in love with Adam. He was a man of few words but I loved the challenge of drawing him out, discovering his inner thoughts.'

After a while she realised the downside of the strong, silent type. It was always her that would drive the conversation forward. Adam only ever spoke one or two sentences at a time. He rarely volunteered anything.

'His silence began to get on my nerves. One night I was really frustrated with him. I decided to try something. We were at our usual Chinese restaurant and I wondered how long it would take him to say something, without me starting the conversation first. We sat there in total silence, sharing a crispy seaweed starter. He didn't say a word through the duck. And I was still waiting when I was finishing the pineapple fritter dessert.

'I got angrier and angrier. Adam finally spoke. He said, "Let's get the bill. Hey, I really enjoyed that. It's great to just appreciate the food, without feeling we have to fill the silence with inane chatter." I was totally stunned, then I exploded at him.'

The relationship ended that evening.

This is an example of a girl who didn't know herself and what she needed. Tina didn't realise just how important talking was to her. She was someone who loved to connect with people through discussion, not someone who was just happy to hear her own voice. She needed a partner who was full of conversation.

WHY SELF-AWARENESS IS MORE IMPORTANT THAN EVER TODAY

We live in a world where you're encouraged to be an individual. You're encouraged to follow your own distinct path in life. You have a vast amount of choice in how to live and you are free to be what you want. You can be an atheist, a Christian, a Muslim, right wing, left wing, a loner, a partygoer, gay, straight, a marathon runner, a couch potato, a drinker, a teetotaller. And it's all fine.

This great diversity in modern life is a good thing. We are free to be who what we want. It's this variety that makes life richer. But it brings its own challenges when it comes to choosing a partner. You will meet, as a matter of routine, men who are very different from you. You could easily fall in love with one of them. But because of your differences, you may be totally incompatible.

In the past, there was less chance of ending up with a guy who was totally different to you. Suppose you were a parlourmaid in Victorian times. You would have had little interaction with your upper-class employers and would usually have only mixed with other servants. From the age of twelve, you would have worked from six in the morning to eleven at night, with a few hours off work on a Sunday afternoon and one free day each month. There was no expectation of moving to a different path in life and the young men that you met would likely be delivery boys or servants, similar in expectations and daily life. You would almost certainly marry within your own station in life, no matter what romantic fiction may say! You would then be a housewife and mother with no independent way of earning and your husband would be the boss. Neither of you had many choices in how you ran your lives.

Dealing with the vast choice you have today requires self-awareness. The range of eligible men ranges far wider than the choice between different fellow servants. Choice requires us to understand our own minds.

DOES 'EQUAL, BUT DIFFERENT' REALLY WORK?

We live in a world where we are free and equal. We are encouraged to believe we can make anything work. Have you seen the film *Pretty Woman*, a love story in which a rich, ruthless businessman falls in love with a poor, quirky sex worker? The story encourages us to believe two people with very different lifestyles can make a blissfully happy couple.

We are so accustomed to the idea that very different people can connect that we don't even blink when we read about Bella choosing between two men utterly different to herself. One is a 107-year-old wealthy vampire and the other a poverty-stricken Quileute werewolf.

In fiction, sharp contrasts make dramatic stories, but in reality, most successful relationships are between two people who have a lot in common.

Of course relationships can work if people are very different. If one or both of you are very willing to compromise, it can work. But people mostly find this a struggle. Research has shown that long-term happy couples are similar to each other.

 Jazz is a 22-year-old guitarist who met Alan at a live music night at her local bar.

'We were both into the same bands. We talked non-stop for about two hours, about music mostly. It was my passion and it was his passion.'

But they were quite different people. Alan was brought up to work very hard. He saw his parents scraping a living and he wanted something different. He was ambitious, and wanted his own business empire one day. Jazz was more of a dreamer, happy to get by earning just enough to support herself with her guitar.

'My parents were university lecturers. They weren't exactly hippies, but they always told me that material things aren't the path to happiness. I totally agree with them that chasing wealth is the wrong way to live.'

Jazz is interested in alternative therapies and her spirituality is based on New Age ideas. 'I don't believe in God as such. There's some kind of power out there, but I don't believe in a God rewarding and punishing us.

But Alan was a committed Christian. He believed what organised religion told him to believe.'

Their lifestyles were also very different. He was driven, impatient, and liked order and tidiness. Jazz didn't care about clutter and was happy 'going with the flow'. She was creative, whereas Alan was very down to earth and practical. Alan's dream was a penthouse flat in London, her dream was living on communal smallholding in the country.

Despite these differences, they fell in love.

Relationships like these between two very different people happen all the time. Often, one common bond – music, in the case of Jazz and Alan – is enough to override other lesser incompatibilities. In the early months of the relationship the couple had a great time together, focused around their shared passion and the overwhelming emotions of falling in love, which swamp any consideration of the differences that seem minor in comparison.

But life together is about far more than one or two major passions. The mundane details of life – the daily routine, the way to relax on weekday evenings, the attitude to money, and so on – are also important in a long-term relationship. Differences that once seemed minor irrelevances can become more important as a relationship develops.

It took five years and one baby before it dawned on Jazz and Alan that they weren't suited to each other. Their shared interest in music couldn't overcome their differences.

'Alan was out all the time. He worked dawn to dusk, just because he had this ambition to be really rich. He kept claiming he was doing it for me, but I totally knew

it was all about him. I told him I wanted him home, to be together and to care for baby Mai and to chill out with some music. I couldn't talk to him. I wanted to talk about ideas, art, thought, dreams; all he wanted to talk about was how much money we had in the bank, or whether we needed double glazing.'

They argued continually because of the differences in their personalities.

'We argued over where to live. We argued over the mess in the house. We argued about me playing guitar in my band. The worst one was about whether Mai should be christened – that argument carried on non-stop for about a month. I was like, you think our daughter must be sworn into organised religion before she can even talk?'

Once the relationship came under stress, it was doomed by their differences.

'I knew for months we should never have got together, but kept trying to make it work. I would have put up with it if I thought there was a way forward, even though I was sick to death of being stuck at home, miserable, and my creativity was stifled. But I just knew we couldn't live together for the rest of our lives. And Alan knew it, too.'

You need to be aware of the culture you come from, your deeply held beliefs, your world view. Many people just aren't aware of their own deeply held values until they painfully clash with their partner and it's too late. Many people don't know themselves properly until they learn from bitter experience.

WHAT WILL MAKE YOUR BOYFRIEND UNHAPPY?

Here's a question that you may not have given much thought to: what aspects of yourself could make a man unhappy?

You probably think quite well of yourself, and don't dwell on your shortcomings too much. But what about your negative side?

It may be hard to believe, but there are aspects of your personality that some men would find difficult. Not all men, just some. This isn't because there's anything wrong with you. But because all humans are different, some of your personality traits could really clash with someone else's.

For example, suppose you are someone who's particular about hygiene and tidiness, comfortable only in clean, orderly surroundings. You feel time spent scrubbing and sorting is time well spent. What would happen if you fell in love with a man who couldn't care less about untidiness and who feels a morning spent cleaning the bathroom is a morning he might as well have been dead?

If you moved in together, your complaining and cleaning up around him would make him unhappy. He would feel the pressure to be someone he's not and feel guilty whenever he left his stuff around. And if he's unhappy with you, it'll make you unhappy.

It's nothing to do with wrong or right, fault or blame. There are plenty of men who like to be tidy and whose dream girl is someone who likes a clean kitchen, too.

What's important is whether you are aware of yourself. Let's take Bella's example.

Bella made Edward unhappy. He suffered hugely in their relationship. Bella was a girl who was careless of her own safety. Self-sacrifice was part of her nature. She almost seemed to relish the idea of sacrificing her life for others. She wasn't in the least bit safety conscious. She wandered off into strange dark streets alone. She hung out with slavering werewolves. Poor Edward spent all his time worrying about her and rescuing her. Edward was an unhappy guy whose only joy was in Bella being alive, yet she was careless about her life.

Throughout the *Twilight* saga, Bella really didn't recognise how much Edward suffered because of her lackadaisical attitude to safety. It even ruined their honeymoon. Edward was upset about the bruising she accidentally sustained during their first night together, and Bella was annoyed with him for being so worried. She didn't truly understand the way he felt. Edward's concerned attitude was much healthier than Bella's. If a man causes you bruising, whether accidental or not, he should be worried. And so should you.

Bella's self-sacrificing nature made him unhappy and this backfired on her. They had rows about her lack of self-preservation.

Luckily, Bella had the option of becoming an immortal vampire, thus solving the problem of physical harm. If not, Edward may well have tired of being so unhappy and stressed all the time.

Your boyfriend may be good for you, but are you good for him? Understanding what you bring to a relationship is vital. You may be aware of the positives you have to contribute, but you also need to perceive the challenges you create.

CRUELTY-FREE LEARNING

One way to acquire self-awareness is through pain. Like Tina (the girl who fell in love with the strong, silent Adam) or Jazz (who fell in love with the ambitious Alan) you can learn your lesson by going out with an unsuitable guy and experiencing the heartache of finding out he can't fulfil your needs. Then you can go through a messy break-up and talk about it with your friends. You can start figuring out what went wrong, and why you weren't suited. You can draw lessons from the relationship about yourself and what you need. You can develop insight and understanding about yourself from the murky, confusing and often surprisingly painful world of relationships.

But you don't have to do it like this.

People commonly believe pain is a good teacher. You often hear people saying 'She had to go through it herself to learn' or 'She had to make her own mistakes'.

Well, it's one way to learn. But it's not the best way. It's much better to learn without any pain at all!

Pain hurts. It's best avoided if you can. Learning through painful mistakes is a foolish option if there's an alternative. Why not learn without pain? Or if you insist on learning through pain, at least make it someone else's.

After all, you're happy to do this in other areas of your life. If you wanted to learn whether a wasp sting was worse than a bee sting, would you go out and stick your hand in a wasps' nest and then your other hand in a bees' nest? Or would you go and look it up on the Internet? If you wanted to learn whether a firm was trustworthy, would you give them money and see if you got ripped off? Or would you find out how they treated other customers?

These are minor pains. The pain of a bee sting and the annoyance of being ripped off is nothing to the amount of agony a really bad relationship can cause. Emotional hurt is arguably worse than physical hurt. After painful break-ups people often say things like they'd rather have a tooth pulled out without anaesthetic than go through that again.

Think of the torture Bella endured when Edward left her in *New Moon*. With her skill as a writer Stephenie Meyer conveys a vivid picture of Bella's emotional suffering. And she isn't exaggerating. As you may know, being dumped by someone you adore really is that bad.

But there is another reason that pain-free learning is better.

When you learn through pain, you learn fear. And fear is not a good teacher. Fear brings problems of its own. In other words, it gives you emotional baggage.

If you learn a lesson through an incredibly painful relationship, it will leave you lacking in confidence. Nervous of making old mistakes, you'll be more likely to blunder into new ones. So although you've learned your lesson, you bring a whole load of hang-ups to your next relationship.

YOUR PERSONAL BAGGAGE

You don't need to have been in a bad relationship to have baggage. Even the most well-adjusted people have some sort of personal problems as they embark on a relationship. It's likely you've had a few negative experiences that have shaped the way you feel.

Baggage is a good word for it. You have collected a burden that weighs you down, the burden of your negative experiences with people. You carry it round with you, then when you get into a relationship you sometimes dump it on your guy. And hope he'll carry it for you.

Having some baggage isn't necessarily a problem. If you have a good awareness of your baggage, and can shoulder it OK, then you'll be fine. But if you land all your problems on a guy he just might crack under the strain.

Just because you have some baggage it does not mean you are sick, or need to be 'cured'. Having personal problems is perfectly normal. We humans are very emotional creatures. Everyone has something that bothers them. Modern life is tough on your emotions.

WHY MODERN LIFE CAUSES PERSONAL PROBLEMS

1) Today's family

You were brought up by probably only one or two caregivers, an unnatural situation compared to most of human history. In the past, families lived closely together, so there were always other relatives around to help look after the children. The pressure cooker of the modern, small family is not necessarily a healthy one. Your caregivers were solely responsible for you, putting more stress on them. There was no escape for you if their parenting was less than satisfactory. There is an old saying, 'It takes a village to raise a child'; children probably thrive best if the whole community cares for them, not just family members. But nowadays many families live in isolation from the people around them.

2) Artificial childhood
You were treated as a child for too long. The period of childhood is extended in modern life – you are forced into a powerless role even though you are physically grown up. You have adult needs for freedom and sex and self-determination, but you have to play the child until you are 18. You may bring this anger, resentment and rebellion into adult life.

3) Too many tough decisions
You have a huge amount of choice in modern life. Research shows increased choice doesn't bring contentment, it breeds dissatisfaction and anxiety.

4) Competitiveness
You have to compete with many human beings for your studies or your job. You have to prove yourself against others from an early age. It's all too easy to conclude you are not good enough.

5) Pressure to be beautiful
There are beautiful faces surrounding us on our TV screens, at the cinema, in adverts. Before the mass media, encountering a truly stunning woman would be rare. But with these images everywhere, we compare ourselves with them and many of us feel we fall short.

Sometimes life feels like a beauty contest that most of us have no chance of winning. Beautiful women are idolised. You can even become rich from nothing other than good looks. Today many girls equate their worth with their physical appearance.

6) Inequality

You are led to believe that we all have equal value as human beings. Yet some people are a lot richer than you, with nicer possessions and more holidays than you. You may feel unhappy about this. You see yourself as just as worthy as them. In times past, people accepted their station in life – they would have seen rich people as their 'betters'. People that wanted more were stamped down, seen as trying to get 'above themselves'. But now, inequality makes us feel stressed, envious and dissatisfied.

7) Loss of meaning

You are likely to be cooped up inside all day, away from the natural world. You have to do repetitive, dull or seemingly pointless study or work. Rewards can be remote from effort.

Today, many girls are looking for more than just love from a guy. They are looking for a solution to their lives. This is too much of a burden to put on a man. All he can do is love you. A relationship won't necessarily be the answer you want it to be.

Are you looking just for love or are you looking for a solution to your problems? How much are you looking to a guy to solve your need for self-esteem, meaning and purpose, security, safety, to simplify your choices, to help sort out the confusion in your life?

Let's look at Bella...

CHAPTER 10

BELLA'S SELF-AWARENESS

DID BELLA KNOW HERSELF?

Bella had major emotional baggage. She was looking for a solution to her life. She knew she wasn't particularly happy, but she didn't have a whole lot of insight into why this was, where it came from and what she could do about it.

When Bella arrived in Forks she was depressed and lonely. She was awkward and lacked confidence. She wasn't able to relate to others – she saw herself as different from the rest of the human race. Bella is not unusual. She is a believable portrait of a young twenty-first-century girl. Many of us can relate to these feelings of isolation and unhappiness.

BELLA'S SELF-ESTEEM

Having a healthy sense of your own worth is vital for a happy life. But before Edward and Jacob, Bella did not think very highly of herself.

Self-esteem is how much you value yourself and how worthwhile you feel compared with other people. You learn about yourself from the way people treat you. If people behave as if you are a valuable and important person, then you'll have a healthy level of self-esteem.

Bella learned about herself from her fellow students at her high school in Phoenix. In this highly competitive world she was always falling short. Where Bella grew up, other young people valued beauty, riches and sporting ability. Bella had none of these things. When Bella sees the vampires for the first time in the school cafeteria, she is fascinated by their beauty. She sees Rosalie's gorgeous hair and figure, and her reaction is to say that any girl near Rosalie would take a hit on her self-esteem.

But being in the same room with someone beautiful will only affect your self-esteem if you believe your worth depends on your looks. Much of *Twilight* emphasises beauty. Many words are devoted to describing the physical charms of the vampires. Bella often mentions how inferior she feels because of her appearance. One of the reasons she longs to be a vampire is to attain their standard of beauty. Her self-esteem is tied up with her looks.

Like many places in the world, in Phoenix there was a pecking order that depended on wealth. Bella had little money, so she had little status. The people at Bella's high school in Phoenix valued athletic ability. Being great at sports was one way of getting admiration and status. Bella's clumsiness and lack of talent made physical education a torture for her. Being humiliated like this did not do her self-esteem any good.

BELLA'S LACK OF PURPOSE

One of the things that marks us humans out from other living creatures is our craving to have a sense of meaning or direction in our lives. Most of us have our eyes set on the future. Now that most of us are lucky enough not to have to worry about surviving from day to day, we are free to think about the point of our existence. For most people, having meaningful goals is important for our sense of well-being and satisfaction. For some, these might be short-term goals – they only look for an easy life and immediate pleasure. Others have a grand plan for their lives.

Before Edward, Bella had no plans. She had no sense of direction and her life had little meaning. Her greatest wish was not to cause problems for others. She goes to school, but there is no sense of purpose. She is cooped up in class being taught things she has already learned. She has no sense of what it's all for.

BELLA'S RELATIONSHIPS WITH OTHERS

Charlie, Bella's father, struggles when relating to others. He only had one close relationship – with Bella's mother – and never really recovered when it ended.

Bella is similar. She never feels she belongs or that people understand her. She doesn't really try to get close, and is often not really 'there' when spending time with others. When she's with Jessica, her gossipy classmate, she just 'tunes out'. She doesn't try to connect with or seek out like-minded companions. She didn't have close friends in Phoenix. When she moves to Forks she doesn't carry on any relationship from Phoenix, apart from the one with her mother.

Bella has some self-awareness – she knows that like Charlie she has problems relating to people, but has little idea of what she can do about it.

It is important for people to feel they belong. Humans are social and closeness to others is vital for well-being.

BELLA'S LONELINESS

There are two types of loneliness. There is the loneliness that comes from being physically isolated from others; when there are literally no people around you. This is highly distressing for most people, which is why solitary confinement is used as one of the worst punishments.

The second type is more common. You can also feel lonely, even if you have people in your life, if you do not feel connected to the people around you. This is almost as bad as solitary confinement. If you feel emotionally isolated from the rest of the human race, you will be miserable.

Bella experiences both types of loneliness. To begin with she is in a state of semi solitary confinement – she has no friends near her and her father is often out of the house or leaving her alone in her room. And she feels she is disconnected from all other people.

Bella cries herself to sleep at the beginning of the story. She plans for these crying 'jags' to take place in private. It doesn't occur to her to seek emotional support. She keeps her deepest, most personal emotions to herself. This is a sign of her isolation from the rest of the human race. Many girls would seek comfort, but Bella bottles it all up. There is no one she could turn to. She can't go to her mother Renee, as it is Bella's habit to protect her. She knows Renee would be upset if she found out her daughter was unhappy, so she hides her emotions. And she can't turn to Charlie, who couldn't cope with her emotions either. There is no one else.

BELLA'S FEARS

Before Edward and Jacob, Bella was consumed with anxiety. Her fears were all about people. When she arrived at Forks she was even nervous about being with her own father. She was terrified of meeting new people at school. Many people are anxious in new social situations, but Bella's fears are extreme. Again, she faces them alone. She tells no one how nervous she feels. She hides her vulnerabilities from those closest to her. She was aware she had a problem in relating to people, but kept it to herself. She was not aware that this unwillingness to confide in others was an important part of her problem.

BELLA'S LACK OF INSTINCT FOR SELF-PRESERVATION

Despite all her fears, when it really mattered Bella had no instinct for responding to real danger. She had been given clear information by Edward that he was dangerous. He told her he wanted to murder her and drink her blood. She should have felt fear, but she didn't. Bella was aware that this didn't make sense.

The fear reaction is a protective mechanism. It kicks in to save your life. If you are under threat, adrenalin streams through your body, causing your heart to pound, your mind to sharpen and your muscles to tense up, ready to fight, freeze or run.

The fact that Bella's fear did not kick in when her life was under threat is a sign that something was very wrong.

THE BAGGAGE FROM BELLA'S PAST

Much of Bella's unhappiness has its roots in her childhood. Her emotional needs hadn't really been met by her parents.

Her mother Renee was impulsive and childlike, so from an early age Bella was forced into the role of parenting her own mother. And her father Charlie was no better. He was an isolated, emotionally distant man unable to respond to Bella in the way she needed. Again, with her father, Bella assumed the role of caregiver, cooking all his meals.

Not only does Bella assume practical responsibilities for her parents, but she assumes responsibility for their emotional well-being, too. Bella doesn't call them Mom or Dad, but Renee and Charlie. This shows us how little she sees them in the parental role.

She was so used to meeting the needs of others that caregiving became a way of life. Looking after others was her way of getting her emotional needs met, a way to feel close to people, to feel good about herself and to feel important to others. But the problem was she had no sense of what her own needs were. It was not just caregiving. It crossed the line into self-sacrifice.

✹ THE POWER OF THE LAMB ✹

Girls often fall into the giving or healing role, and are more willing than men to put their own needs aside for the good of others.

Why is this? Some say it is our biology; that we have evolved to have a stronger instinct to nurture than men. Women of all societies do most of the child care.

Others say it's because of the way we are brought up in society. Before she can even talk a little girl will probably be given a doll to play with. Girls are taught to care for others and to put their own needs to one side.

The power to soothe, heal and nurture is the one power that women are encouraged to show. When a young girl is deprived of care, this instinct to nurture often becomes exaggerated and she becomes a carer for others. Nurturing others is one way to feel close to people, to feel loved and have a sense of personal power and importance.

The image of the lion falling in love with the lamb sums this up. The lamb has the power to transform the lion. The lamb is important and powerful enough to change his aggressive impulses. While it seems that the lion is the one in charge, in fact the lamb has something far more powerful.

Life for most people is about keeping a good balance between giving to others and taking from others. Bella grew up feeling her own needs were not important and that it was much more important for her to give.

At the beginning of the *Twilight* series, Bella is a girl who is miserable, anxious, lonely, directionless and has a penchant for self-sacrifice...

CUE EDWARD

Edward is another lonely, unhappy soul – and one with a taste for human blood.

He had wandered the earth for 90 years, hating himself, unable to see the point of his existence. Edward is an exaggerated version of how many troubled men feel. Typically, when males have emotional difficulties, it doesn't show itself in excessive self-sacrifice and a need to nurture other people. It more commonly comes out in the form of destructive or aggressive behaviour.

Edward has to fight murderous impulses every day of his life. He loathes himself. His life is dark. He has problems in his relationships with women. He has never fallen in love with any girl.

And then Bella and Edward meet. They connect. Their love for each other flames brightly, dispelling the darkness. The burden of their emotional baggage disappears. The power of their love conquers all. They were two individuals with major personal, emotional and relationship difficulties. But – in fiction – love dramatically solves all these.

Bella was carrying the baggage of her unmet emotional needs. She needed a guy to love and look after her. Her mother had not provided a sense of security and protection and the love she received from Charlie was distant and unaffectionate. Neither parent was capable of providing the type of emotional support she needed. Edward provided this in spades. He was the strong, capable caregiver she'd never had.

Edward had needs of his own. Edward was looking for meaning in his life; he needed to find a purpose to his existence, and someone to help him conquer his murderous impulses. Bella provided all this. She healed the tortured dark hero's wounds. The dangerous, brooding Edward was really a wonderful, loving man. Love was the answer to their problems and they both lived happily ever after.

The characters follow the rules of romance, to provide us with a highly enjoyable story. It's not realistic, but that's one of the points of reading fiction. It is an escape from real life.

But if Edward was a real man, he would not have solved Bella's personal unhappiness. If he was following the rules of human nature, not the rules of romantic fiction, he would have continued with his controlling ways and one day he would have given in to his violent impulses.

The idea of the 'lamb' sums Bella up. She is gentle and soft, and for thousands of years, lambs have been an animal used in sacrifice. She was a lamb 'ready for the slaughter'.

Stephenie Meyer has drawn characters and relationships that are in many ways very psychologically true to life. There is much wisdom and depth in the way Stephenie Meyer portrays the relationships between Bella, the Cullens, Jacob, Charlie, Renee, and the rest of the Quileutes and the students at Forks High School.

In real life there are plenty of Edwards, Jacobs and Bellas. There are plenty of lambs – selfless girls yearning for someone they can pour their love into. There are plenty of lions, too – aggressive, complicated guys longing to be soothed and healed. But what really happens when a loving, self-sacrificing girl tries to heal the wounded, dangerous man? What does the lion/lamb dynamic look like in real life?

It is the dynamic behind abusive relationships.

If Bella and Edward were real human beings, the end of the story would not be a happy one. A predatory man cannot solve a girl's emotional problems, and a girl's love cannot change a man's violent impulses. The real-life story ends in violence, sometimes death.

MEET THE REAL-LIFE BELLA

Izzy was introduced to Keiran by her friend Philippa. 'The moment I saw him my heart fluttered. He was tall and handsome, with a dark brooding look. I thought he was fascinating.'

At 31 he was eight years older than her and Philippa told her he had a reputation for being hot-tempered. 'Our first date was at an expensive Italian restaurant. I bought a cut-out black dress for it and Keiran saw me and said, 'Wow!' He said he'd never seen anyone look more stunning. No one had ever said that about me. I'm not the kind of girl who inspires strong feeling in others. We talked for hours – he'd had an exciting life: the army and then setting up his own business running outdoor courses. But all the time I could sense a sadness running through him. I longed to find out why.'

Even on this first date Keiran revealed something of his personality. He joked about how he did time in an army jail for fighting.

'On our second date I discovered why he often looked moody. I asked why he'd left the army. "I got diabetes," he said. "They made me leave." He described how much he detested being a diabetic, having to inject himself several times a day and be careful with his diet. From that moment on, I had the urge to care for him.'

Izzy had always liked to put others first. Her older brother, Rick, was academically gifted and talented at tennis. Her parents had held high hopes for his future and the whole family dreamed of Rick winning Wimbledon. Throughout her childhood she received praise from her parents for helping with chores, so Rick could be ferried to his tennis tournaments, and it felt quite natural to Izzy that Rick was the centre of attention.

'I never expected to match up to Rick. I'm average. Schoolwork was usually a struggle and I'm hopeless at sports. But I always enjoyed being useful to others and that's what I need for my job. I sell display space for *exhibitions. I love moving heaven and earth to sort out problems for clients and often figure out what they want before they realise it.'* In fact, Izzy was so good she won her company's salesperson of the year award. *'Not sure I deserved it. Anyway, compared to playing in international tennis tournaments it's not anything to write home about.'*

As the relationship developed, Keiran kept saying how gorgeous and special she was. As she had low self-esteem, Izzy found it odd as well as thrilling to hear it. She soon became hooked.

When she first took Keiran to meet her family she realised he was perceptive. *'Driving home afterwards, he pointed out how my parents constantly talked about Rick. They never once asked about my work. I hadn't even expected them to, but Keiran said, "It's not right. Your parents should have treated you equally to Rick, no matter what his amazing talent was. That's why you lack confidence." I realised Keiran was right and cried on his shoulder that night.'*

Keiran opened up to her, too. He'd had an unhappy childhood. *'My dad bullied my mum,'* he told her. *'And he was the same to me. He used to call me a runt and said beatings would toughen me up. I got him, though, when I was fourteen. He went to slap me and I landed a right jab on his nose. Hard. I heard it break. I expected to get a good hiding but he just left the room, clutching his bloody nose. Never talked about it. And he never hit me again.'*

'I was incredibly proud that Keiran trusted me enough to reveal his private demons,' said Izzy. *'He told me he went into the army because he never wanted to feel weak and vulnerable again. But he admitted he ended up feeling small and unimportant, just another cog in the army machine.'*

For three months Izzy and Keiran were inseparable. They propped up each other's self-esteem, and they both found the love and acceptance they craved. But Keiran had moods. 'He would be snappy if I was late or couldn't see him because I was taking clients out for the evening. He always apologised afterwards, though. It was because his low blood sugar made him irritable. I began to realise how much he hated his diabetes – he couldn't stand the restrictions on his life and saw it as a threat to his masculinity. He rebelled against it by eating the wrong foods and taking his insulin late.' *She gave reassurance that his illness didn't detract from him in the slightest in her eyes.*

After several months of loved-up bliss, Izzy arranged a girl's night out for her best friend Philippa's birthday. 'When I told Keiran I was going out, he went moody. He said, "There better not be any men around who'll make a play for you." When I saw him the next day he asked what I'd worn for the evening. I told him it was my favourite black dress and he said, "What, the one you wore the night we met?" I said yes and he glared at me, raging on that it was a "mean trick" to play on him. He stormed out.'

Four hours later, Keiran came back, full of apologies. 'It all came pouring out. He said he was only behaving like that because he was insecure, and he loved me so much he was terrified of losing me, and he didn't feel good enough for me because of his diabetes. He swore he'd never speak like that again. "It's not that I don't trust you," he said. "It's other men I don't trust. Not around someone as gorgeous as you." I was overwhelmed with compassion because he seemed so vulnerable. I could *see the frightened little boy in him, the boy who'd been mercilessly bullied by his father. I had never felt so close to another human being.'*

They moved in together. 'I thought he'd feel more secure if we were together more, and it seemed that way for a few months. Then I went away for my work's annual conference. Keiran was moody about it but I could live with that. All men have their drawbacks.'

But she came back late from the conference. Keiran greeted her coldly, then snapped at her for being late. He grabbed her suitcase, unzipped it and turned it upside down. 'All my clothes tumbled out. He seized items and began interrogating me. He waved a bra in my face and demanded to know why I'd taken sexy underwear. It was just a bra. Then he slapped my face.

'I was stunned. But Keiran immediately said, "Oh God, what have I done?" He looked horrified. He held me in his arms while I cried. He kept stroking me, repeating how sorry he was. "I'm a monster," he said. "I don't deserve you. I want to protect you, keep you away from men who'd use you." He promised he'd never hurt me again.'

After this incident, they spent ages talking about his insecurities and his childhood. Keiran seemed grateful for her help, and showered her with flowers and romantic presents. He told Izzy she was the only one who truly understood him.

But for the next year the same pattern kept happening. Keiran would get moody and sometimes physical if she was out with friends. Izzy told herself it was no big deal. 'It was usually just a push, or a slap, then Keiran would back down.' He would apologise profusely afterwards and Izzy knew he was tormented and unhappy about *his behaviour. The incidents always ended with Izzy comforting him.*

'I started turning down invitations to go out as they weren't worth the trouble. Everything was fine so long as I was with Keiran all the time.'

She started playing down the amount of contact she had with male customers. 'One night I had to entertain my number one client at an expensive London restaurant. There were four men, but I'd led Keiran to believe there'd be women as well. When I let myself into the house I found Keiran standing there with a face like thunder. "You lied to me," he said. "You said there'd be all women. I saw you. They were all men. And you were flirting with them like a hooker!"

'My heart was thumping with fear but I got angry. "How dare you follow me!" I yelled. "Good job I did," Keiran said. "It proved you can't be trusted."'

Izzy tried to leave the house. 'It was horrible. Keiran was white with anger and I was too tired to take any more. "You're sick!" I shouted. I got out the door but he grabbed my arm and dragged me back in. "You're the sick one," he said. "Lying to me while tarting yourself around."

'He got me by the neck. I slumped to the floor. His strong hands kept squeezing my throat. "Promise you'll never lie to me again," he said. I couldn't even scream. "Promise me," he kept saying. My vision went blurry and I knew I was going to die.

'All of a sudden Keiran let go. He looked shocked and put his head in his hands.

'I could see he was devastated by his behaviour. Instinctively I stepped forward to comfort him. But something was different. I didn't feel the usual compassion.

All I could see was a vision of Kieran kneeling over my dead body, saying sorry for strangling me.

'I turned away and ran out of the house. I never went back.'

This is what happens to relationships in real life when the lamb tries to cure the lion of his aggression. Izzy's story is just one of the many real-life stories of women who fall in love with a guy who at first seems strong and exciting, but is actually controlling and violent. There is no happy ending. The relationship ends with the girl breaking away to save her sanity. Luckily, many manage to escape like Izzy and eventually turn their lives around.

Today, Izzy knows the power of her love cannot cure a man, no matter how much she wishes it. She advises her girlfriends never to take responsibility for trying to change a guy.

But some women in abusive relationships have nothing to say on the subject. They feel ashamed and blame themselves, so keep it secret. Or they are scared to talk. Or they are in denial, telling themselves that a slap is nothing much to worry about or a raised fist is just part of normal life. And for a tragic few, they cannot say anything at all because they are dead, the lambs murdered by their beloved lions, their voices silenced for ever.

TIME TO LIGHTEN THE MOOD

OK, so this is the worst-case scenario. Most people won't get sucked into a dangerous relationship. Hopefully you will avoid a dangerous man.

But bringing a personal unhappiness to a man means you may be less happy with him. Research shows that your own personality is crucial to how you experience relationships. If you're often in negative emotional states – for example, experiencing low mood, anger, anxiety and guilt – you are much more likely to be dissatisfied in your relationship, and to feel that you're not very close to your partner.

Bella was full of negative emotional states, so a girl like Bella is less likely to have a satisfactory relationship.

In reality, your boyfriend cannot be a god for you and sort out your life. He cannot be a therapist for you. You are not paying him by the hour.

If Bella were a real person, her best chance of having a happy love life would be to sort out her own issues before she embarked on a relationship.

But in fiction, we can enjoy the idea that her unhappiness can be solved through love. It's an idea of our times. In the old days, we would have been told to pray or turn to God for help. Nowadays we are encouraged to believe our personal issues and lack of confidence can all be transformed if we meet The One. True Love is seen as the way to earthly bliss.

But it often doesn't work out like that. If you have issues, they don't disappear because you're in a relationship. Girls who are happily in love are likely to have been happy anyway, before they met their guy.

WHAT DOES THIS MEAN FOR FINDING A GREAT RELATIONSHIP?

You need to be aware of what you are bringing to it. If you know yourself, you can accurately judge what you can give to a boyfriend and what you need from him. Knowing yourself can help you pick the right guy.

And you need to be looking for love, just love, not love as an answer to your life. If you think a man is the solution to your life, he'll end up being the problem.

Are you, like Bella, bringing a whole truckload of baggage with you and hoping it will magically disappear when you find true love? Or perhaps you're nothing like Bella, you're perfectly sorted, and perfectly self-aware.

Who are you and what are you looking for in a relationship? Read on to find out more.

CHAPTER 11

INSIGHTS FROM YOUR RELATIONSHIP HISTORY

Who you are depends on your relationships, both past and present.

The people in your life have influenced your mind and emotions. You have been shaped by your parents, brothers and sisters, friends, teachers, boyfriends and classmates.

You can learn a huge amount about yourself by looking at your relationship history. Each important person in your life has made an impact on you, for good or for bad.

As soon as we are born we begin forming relationships with others. As a baby, you could control your parents with smiles and crying and laughter, long before you could communicate verbally. The quality of these relationships, from babyhood right up till now, has shaped how you feel today.

IT'S NOT AN IDEAL WORLD

If life was perfect, your family, friends, peers and teachers would have all treated you wonderfully, and you would have grown up feeling perfectly confident and happy.

If this describes you, turn to the next chapter. In fact, you can throw away the book now. Go on; put it in the nearest bin. You are wasting time sitting here reading this book – just get out there and carry on with your amazing life!

Do you know anybody like this? Of course not. Nobody has been brought up in an ideal world, because this isn't one. Most people have had experiences in their relationships which have influenced them – not always for the better.

All of us, at some time or other, have been shamed, ignored, ridiculed, rejected, neglected, hurt, bullied, abused, ignored, belittled, laughed at, held in contempt, persecuted. And many of us feel that we have never been loved, liked or admired enough.

Most people recover from these experiences with no ill effects. But these experiences may leave their mark. And they will influence what you bring to your relationships. Do you have any baggage from the past which may be affecting the way you behave in relationships?

You need to look at your past to help you find out.

HOW CAN YOU LEARN FROM YOUR RELATIONSHIPS?

By asking the right questions. Insight and understanding are attained when you know what to ask. Questions open up your mind, help you to make links, connections, and make sense of the confusion. That's why psychologists are always asking questions.

This chapter includes some of the questions psychologists use. You can think about them by yourself, or write down what comes into your mind, or talk with a close friend or family member. Writing answers down or talking with someone you trust are usually better than just thinking about the answers yourself. If you talk with someone else about these very personal questions, make sure you can trust the other person to keep your conversations private.

Let's start at the beginning, with your relationships with your mother and father. If you weren't brought up by your natural parents, think about the person who was the closest to a mother or father figure for you.

Early on in life, you learn who you are and how to relate to other people from the people who love you. The way you were cared for has influenced the person you have become today. This is not about blaming your family; it's about understanding yourself better. There's nobody on the planet that's had a perfect upbringing with perfect parents. Most families have their difficulties and their strengths. This exercise is not meant to be about focusing on the negatives, or looking for problems where none exist. When thinking about these questions, recognise the positive aspects of your experiences, too.

YOUR RELATIONSHIP WITH YOUR MOTHER AND/OR STEPMOTHER

The material for this one could fill a library! Mothers are important. The way she cared for you in your early years shaped the way your mind and emotions developed. Your mother gives you your first experience of love.

The nature of your relationship with your mother is likely to have a big impact on what you bring to adult relationships. Ask yourself the following questions. They do not cover absolutely everything; use them as a start for opening up a line of thinking. It may be better to talk about family members with a close friend, rather than a relative. It is often difficult to talk about these topics with someone who also has an emotional involvement. If you do talk about family relationships in this in-depth way with other relatives, they may have strong feelings themselves and find it difficult to keep your conversations confidential.

- How much did you feel loved by your mother?
- How did she show her feelings for you?
- How protected did you feel by her?
- What, if anything, was missing from your relationship?

- What would you love to get from her that you haven't had so far?
- What emotions does she typically trigger in you?
- What do you dislike about your mother?
- In what ways are you like your mother?
- In what ways are you different?
- How much did she help/not help you make the transition from child to young woman?
- What fights did you have with your mother, and what do they say about your relationship?
- How did she make you feel about yourself?
- How secure did you feel in your relationship with her?
- What has your relationship with your mum taught you about being loved?

Your conclusions

When you have thought, written or talked about your answers to these questions, see if you can draw some conclusions. Have a go at filling in the blanks:

My relationship with my mother was:
It has affected me in this way:
What this might mean for my relationships with men:

What Bella's answers might have been

It's difficult to think about your relationships unless you have something to compare them with. If you only have your own experience to go on, it's hard to make judgements. So here is what Bella might have put:

My relationship with my mother was: 'A role reversal. Renee didn't look after me in the way a parent would. Although I knew she loved me, she didn't make herself responsible for my day-to-day physical needs, to protect me, to shield me as far as possible from negative experiences. Instead, I was the one who did this for her. I always feel responsible for her happiness. I feel guilty if I don't protect her from suffering. I always had to be the strong one.'

It has affected me in this way: 'I guess I never really felt looked after.'

What this might mean for my relationships with men: 'I am in the market for a man who will look after me. I want someone to take care of me for a change. Someone I don't need to look after and who will be the strong one for me.'

YOUR RELATIONSHIP WITH YOUR FATHER AND/OR STEPFATHER

Your father is your first experience of love from a man. Many people assume having a father figure is not as important for girls as boys. You often hear people saying, 'A boy needs a man around.' This is true. A boy does learn how to be a man from a father figure.

But a father figure is just as important for girls. Girls need to learn about men, too. You learn how to be loved by a man from your father. As a girl, if you have no father figure or if your father treats you badly you are more susceptible to having bad relationships with men in later life.

Having bad relationships is a very serious problem. It can cause loneliness, depression and can even be dangerous. For example, a disastrous relationship with a man could result in you getting pregnant and being abandoned, or you could have your self-esteem destroyed.

Being discriminating about men is a vital skill. A girl neglected by her father is more likely to be flattered by male admiration, and may not be discriminating enough. If you are treated badly by your father you are more likely to end up being treated badly by men in later life, because bad treatment just feels normal to you.

A happy relationship with a loving dad is a good basis for going on to have loving and fulfilling relationships with men as an adult.

Think, write or talk about these questions with someone you trust:

- How much did you feel loved by your father?
- How did he show his feelings for you?
- How protected did you feel by him?
- What, if anything, was missing from your relationship?
- What would you love to hear or get from him that you haven't had so far?
- What emotions does he typically trigger in you?
- What do you dislike about your father?
- In what ways are you similar to your father?
- In what ways are you different?
- How did he help you/not help you make the transition from child to young woman?
- What fights did you have with your father, and what do they say about your relationship?
- How secure did you feel in your relationship with him?
- How did he make you feel about yourself?
- What has your relationship with your dad taught you about being loved by a man?

Your conclusions

When you have thought, written, or talked about your answers to these questions, see if you can draw some conclusions. Have a go at filling in the blanks:

My relationship with my father was:
It has affected me in this way:
What this might mean for my relationships with men:

What Bella's answers might have been

My relationship with my father was: *'Emotionally distant and unaffectionate. Although I knew that deep down he cared for me, Charlie didn't respond to me much. He was embarrassed by emotion, and I felt uncomfortable about showing emotion, too. I never felt close to him.'*

It has affected me in this way: *'I am very like Charlie. I am uncomfortable with people. I have never experienced what it's like to feel close to and to have physical affection from a man. I am not confident a guy could ever love me and respond to me emotionally.'*

What this might mean for my relationships with men: *'I don't know how to be close to a man. I find it hard to believe a guy would want me. I don't know how close relationships work. I may be vulnerable to the wrong type of guy. I might be needy in relationships as I'm too desperate for love.'*

YOUR RELATIONSHIPS WITH YOUR BROTHERS AND SISTERS

Your relationships with your siblings will shape you, too. Parents usually make comparisons between their children, and siblings compare themselves to each other.

Once you've had a label slapped on you, it can take on a life of its own. For example, imagine your sister is known in the family as 'the pretty one'. She's likely to live up to this – to take more care of her appearance, clothes and make-up – so it becomes even more true. And if you have been labelled 'the clever one' it will probably become truer, too. You will study hard and pay less attention to your appearance.

Family life with your siblings will have helped form your personality.

Think, write or talk about these questions with someone you trust:

- What comparisons were made between you and your siblings? Did any of these labels stick?
- How do your brothers or sisters make you feel about yourself?
- What, if anything, was missing from your relationships with them?
- What would you love to hear or get from your siblings that you haven't had so far?
- What emotions do they typically trigger in you?
- How valued do you feel in your relationships with them?
- In what ways are you similar to your brothers or sisters?
- In what ways are you different?
- What fights did you have with them, and what does this say about your relationships with them?

Your conclusions

When you have thought, written, or talked about your answers to these questions, see if you can draw some conclusions. Have a go at filling in the blanks:

My relationships with my siblings were:
It has affected me in this way:
What this might mean for my relationships with men:

Bella was an only child, so instead we can use another example. Remember Izzy from the last chapter, the real-life Bella? She was the salesperson who fell in love with the exciting but dangerous Keiran, who put his hands round her throat. These were her answers:

My relationships with my siblings were: 'Complicated. Although I adored my older brother Rick, I always felt in his shadow. He was incredibly clever and athletic, everything I wasn't. My parents thought the world of him. I worshipped him, too.'

It has affected me in this way: 'I don't feel very worthwhile. I'm not as important as most people and I'm not special.'

What this might mean for my relationships with men: 'I will look for validation from a man. I'll struggle to feel equal in a relationship with a man, because I instinctively feel inferior to men, as I felt to my brother. I may not feel good enough.'

✹ THE MYTH OF THE ONLY CHILD ✹

If you were an only child, then you won't have any baggage about siblings. This is one of the advantages!

But have you heard people say that only children are more likely to be lonely, to be spoiled and selfish, unable to cooperate with others, and to grow up convinced that they are the centre of the universe?

It's likely that you have heard this. You may even believe it yourself. Many people think that being an only child is a negative thing. Lots of parents decide to have a second baby, not because they are particularly desperate to have another, but because they don't want their firstborn to be an only child. They worry about how their first child will grow up.

But studies show there is no evidence for this myth of the selfish, lonely only child. Only children are no lonelier, self-centred, or spoilt than children with siblings. In fact, if anything, the evidence shows only children are better adjusted than children with brothers or sisters. If you are an only child, you are likely to be more motivated and more able to adjust well to new situations.

One reason being an only child is positive could be that your parents can devote more resources and time to you.

So, if you don't have siblings, the next time you hear someone repeating the 'Only Child Myth', you can put them right!

OTHER PEOPLE SHAPE YOU TOO: YOUR SCHOOL FRIENDS, YOUR PEERS…

Some psychologists believe the school friends you grew up with are even more important for your development than your parents. For example, if you move to a new area of the country when you are a child, where the children have a different accent, you are far more likely to end up with the same accent as your friends and not your parents. You will model yourself on the children around you, not your mother or father. This is why children of loving, good parents can still get into trouble. If the kids around you are violent, drug-taking and into crime, you will be more likely to follow suit.

Whether your friends are more important than your parents is controversial, but there is no doubt they affect you. You learn who you are from how your friends or schoolmates treat you. If you go to school and are treated like an outcast, called names or ignored, this will have a huge impact. Even if you get loving treatment at home this might be outweighed by the damage caused at school.

Not being accepted and having no friends is very distressing for most people. When Bella managed to find a peer group where she fitted in (the Cullens) this transformed her emotional life, almost as much as her relationships with Edward and Jacob did. She found care and acceptance from Alice, and a female 'best friend' was what she needed as much as anything. Having the Cullen family to bond with was good for her.

Like Bella, do you struggle with your peer group?

Think, write or talk about these questions with someone you trust:

- How do you get on with your peers?
- How do you compare with them?
- Do you 'fit in'? If not, what are the differences between you and the people around you?
- What messages do you get about yourself from people your own age?
- To what extent are you able to confide in others?
- To what extent does your social circle fulfil your needs?
- What is missing from your relationships with people your own age?

Your conclusions

When you have thought, written, or talked about your answers to these questions, see if you can draw some conclusions. Have a go at filling in the blanks:

My relationship with my friends/schoolmates was:
It has affected me in this way:
What this might mean for my relationships with men:

What Bella's answers might have been

My relationships with my friends/school mates were: 'Not close or supportive. In Phoenix I always felt different to people my own age.

I preferred people in books. I have never fitted in. I don't have a best friend. I hate attention from others.'

It has affected me in this way: 'I am lonely. I have no one to turn to. I assume people won't like me. I don't try to get close to people. I try to avoid people if I can. I don't trust them.'

What this might mean for my relationships with men: 'Because I don't have friends, when I get a boyfriend he will be everything to me. I will look for all my needs for acceptance and closeness from him. This may put too much pressure on the relationship. If he dumps me, I will have nothing, and no one I can turn to who will help me heal my broken heart.'

WHAT IS YOUR RELATIONSHIP PATTERN?

You can learn plenty about yourself from looking at your relationships with your ex-boyfriends. But lots of girls don't learn anything; they go from one unsatisfactory relationship to the next, making the same mistakes again and again, or making new mistakes.

There are often patterns of attraction in relationships with men. The most common patterns of attraction are the three 'R's: the Repeating, the Ricochet and the Random pattern.

The Repeating Pattern

This is where you go for the same kind of guy each time and it doesn't work out, yet you repeat the same mistake without any learning taking place. Bella is a repeater. When Bella was dumped by Edward in *New Moon* she sought refuge in Jacob, another dangerous guy.

The Ricochet

This is the situation where the faults of one man propel you into the arms of another man with the opposite faults.

This can mean going back and forth. Bored by a 'nice guy', you might go for a 'bad boy'. Then, shaken by your experience with a 'bad boy', you might go back into the refuge of the 'nice guy'. And so on.

Or you can lurch between different types of man. Meet Michelle, a 23-year-old pilates instructor. This is her relationship history:

Phil, her first boyfriend was very laid-back – but he was so laid-back he was horizontal. He never wanted to do anything and she had to ring him to get him out of bed each day. She ended it and instead saw…

… Greg, an ambitious, energetic man. But he was ruthless, wasn't very nice to her and always put his work first. He dumped her to move to Japan for his career.

Her next guy, Will, was kind, but not very clever. She realised it wouldn't work out when she complained about the size of the vet's bill for her cat and he said, 'Well, why did you go private, then?'

Fraser was a clever chap, a research scientist, but a commitment-phobe, so cagey about planning for the future with her he wouldn't agree to do anything more than 24 hours ahead. So she began dating…

… Liam, who was committed from the start, but he was so committed that he felt downright clingy.

Michelle ricochets from one type of man to another, like a human pinball. She pings between men, trying to correct the faults of the previous relationship, but finding new ones.

The Random Pattern

Sometimes there is no real relationship pattern. Sometimes a girl will go out with a guy because he happens to come along.

This is the type of girl who doesn't think too deeply about what she's looking for in a man or her motivations for being with him. When you ask this girl why she is going out with him, she shrugs her shoulders and says she doesn't really know. She says, he was around, it just happened.

I call this the 'George Mallory' approach to relationships. George Mallory, the famous mountaineer, was asked why he wanted to climb Mount Everest. He replied, 'Because it's there.' And you might know how that turned out. He fell off the mountain and died. No one will ever know whether he even reached the summit.

The 'because he was there' approach to boyfriends can be similarly unsuccessful.

YOUR EX-BOYFRIENDS

Love can be painful. Maybe you have been lucky and have never been hurt by a boyfriend. But most of us have been hurt at some time or other. Broken hearts do heal, but after healing there may be a difference in you. Your relationships may leave a scar that changes the way you love.

Each serious boyfriend has an impact which may have a bearing on your next relationship. By serious boyfriend, I mean any man who made an impression on your emotions. It's not about the length of time you were with him, but how deeply he affected you.

Look at all your serious ex-boyfriends in turn, and think, write or talk about these questions with someone you trust:

- What first attracted you to him? What does this say about you?
- What aspects of him made the relationship end?
- What did you contribute to the relationship ending?
- What aspects of him did you feel very negative about? What does this say about you?
- What aspects of him did you love or like? What does this say about you?
- Are there patterns in this relationship that have been played out in other relationships with men?
- What similarities are there in your relationship with him and your early relationships (for example, your mother or father)?
- What differences are there in your relationship with him and your early relationships?
- What was missing from this relationship?

Your conclusions

When you have thought, written or talked about your answers to these questions, see if you can draw some conclusions. Have a go at filling in the blanks for each serious boyfriend:

My relationship with my ex-boyfriend was:
It has affected me in this way:
What this might mean for my future relationships with men:

Izzy's answers

My relationship with my ex-boyfriend was: 'Violent. I was attracted by what I thought were signs of strength. What I thought was manly and exciting, was really the signs of aggression. I may be attracted to violent guys and I don't know why. I liked the feeling of closeness and sense of being useful when I helped him with his issues.'

It has affected me in this way: 'Being with Keiran has made me lose my confidence.'

What this might mean for my future relationships with men: 'Having even less confidence in myself can't be a good thing. Maybe I will be even more likely to end up with the wrong type of guy.'

Izzy went for some help. She realised that whilst she was confident at work, in her personal life she was unsure of herself. So it felt good to be with what she thought was a strong man who could guide and protect her. She was attracted to dominant, exciting men. She was a lamb, attracted to a powerful lion.

Her mistake was to see an aggressive man, and to imagine he was a strong man.

Through counselling, she learned her problems had their roots in her early family life. Overshadowed by her brother Rick, she'd grown up feeling unimportant. She had found the best way to get recognition and a sense of self-esteem was by helping others. Her own needs were not priorities. Self-sacrifice became part of her nature.

She had been looking to a man to solve her feelings of powerlessness and low self-esteem. So instead she worked on increasing her sense of personal worth and power, and changing her tendency to sacrifice herself for others. In time she was able to recognise signs of a dangerous man.

✷ **HEALTH WARNING** ✷

If you have a pattern of being attracted to dangerous guys, have a history of abuse, or if these exercises trigger painful emotions which are too much for you to cope with, then you should seek professional support. Please turn to the Where To Go For Help section at the back of the book for some contact information and ideas for where to seek advice and support.

TO SUM UP

A big part of who you are is the sum total of all your past and present relationships. Reflecting on these and how you have been influenced by the past should give you some clues about what you are bringing into a new relationship, so that hopefully you can go into it with your eyes open.

Or perhaps you have realised that you don't have any particular issues – your past has been happy enough and you are a fully confident girl, in a great position to go into a loving relationship.

But you are not just a page, to be written on by other people. Other people may shape you, but they don't define who you are. You are an individual in your own right. What kind of person are you?

CHAPTER 12

HOW TO BE MORE SELF-AWARE: BELLA, EDWARD AND JACOB'S PERSONALITIES

Girls who find true love have great intuition about the kind of guy who'll make them happy. But what does 'great intuition' mean? Part of this intuition is better self-awareness – knowing yourself. Girls who find true love know who they are, so they can recognise their soulmate when they meet him.

In *Eclipse*, Rosalie tells Bella about how she met her soulmate, Emmett. Rosalie says Emmett is the ideal man for her, the person she would have looked for in the first place if she'd have known herself better.

This chapter is about knowing yourself better.

WHAT IS YOUR PERSONALITY?

Psychologists have identified five major elements of personality, known as 'the Big Five':

1) Negative emotions, or 'neuroticism'

People differ in how prone they are to negative emotions. Everyone feels upset sometimes. Life is not always easy for most people and unavoidably there will be times when you are sad, stressed, angry or nervous. But some people are more vulnerable than others.

What about you? Do you, like Bella, suffer from a high level of sadness, stress, anger and anxiety? Grab a pen or pencil, then read these statements and put a cross somewhere along the line depending on what you think is true of you.

I get stressed out easily
Very true..not at all true
I often feel miserable
Very true..not at all true
I worry about things
Very true..not at all true
I am easily disturbed
Very true..not at all true
I change my mood a lot
Very true..not at all true
I get irritated easily
Very true..not at all true

The more your marks are towards the left side of the page, the more you suffer from negative emotions. This isn't a diagnosis and doesn't mean there is anything wrong with you – these all vary in the normal population. If you are a teenager going through the usual stresses and changes of growing up then you are more likely to experience these emotions. But if you are as unhappy as Bella, it might be worth talking to somebody about getting some help.

2) Ability to get on with others, or 'agreeableness'
This aspect of your personality is about how you deal with people. If you are very agreeable, you find it easy to cooperate with others. Harmonising with people is very important to you. You generally like people and have a positive view of human nature.

How agreeable are you?

I am interested in people
Very true...not at all true
I sympathise with others' feelings
Very true...not at all true
I spend time on others
Very true...not at all true
I like to put people at ease
Very true...not at all true
I would rarely insult anyone
Very true...not at all true
I like hearing about problems
Very true...not at all true
I am concerned about others
Very true...not at all true

If your marks are more to the left, then you are high in this personality factor. This means you are likely to get on well with others. If your marks are situated more towards the right, then people are not your focus. There's nothing wrong with this – it just means you have other priorities in life, and making people at ease and happy is not high up on your agenda. Apart from Esme and Carlisle, the Cullens aren't very agreeable (but it's difficult to get a high score on this item if you're a vampire who likes to drink human blood!).

3) Extroversion and introversion
Extroverted people get enjoyment and stimulation from the outside world. In other words, they look outside themselves more. They enjoy being in large groups and tend to get bored and dissatisfied when alone. They tend to be louder and like strong colours. Introverts prefer the inner life. They feel over-stimulated in crowds and noise, and prefer having fewer people

around. They enjoy solitude and quiet, and can think more clearly when alone.

I am the life of the party
Very true...not at all true
I feel comfortable around others
Very true...not at all true
I start conversations
Very true...not at all true
I like talking to different people
Very true...not at all true
I like being the centre of attention
Very true...not at all true
In a group I talk too much
Very true...not at all true
I often start talking to strangers
Very true...not at all true

If most of your crosses are on the right, you are more on the introverted side. Bella is an introvert, whereas Alice is more of an extrovert. If your answers are in the middle, then you have aspects of both, called 'ambiversion'. You can feel very comfortable with quiet and solitude, but also enjoy a good party.

There's nothing wrong with being extroverted or introverted. There are advantages and disadvantages to both, and there is no evidence that one type is happier than the other.

4) Intellectual style, or 'openness to experience'
This part of personality is about the type of intelligence you have. Some people are very imaginative, while others are more down to earth. If you are imaginative, you like thinking abstractly. You are curious about the world and are more likely to be interested

in beauty, art and literature. If you are the down-to-earth type, you prefer to think in a more straightforward way. You view imaginative pursuits as a bit of a waste of time, and prefer a more practical, common-sense approach.

I often have good ideas
Very true...not at all true
I am quick to understand things
Very true...not at all true
I have a rich vocabulary
Very true...not at all true
I spend time reflecting on things
Very true...not at all true
Abstract concepts interest me
Very true...not at all true
I plan before doing anything
Very true...not at all true
I'm not good at practical tasks
Very true...not at all true

If most of your crosses are towards the right, your intellect is of the practical, down-to-earth type – rather like Jacob's. If they are more to the left, you have the imaginative kind of mind, like Bella and Edward. Bella has a vivid imagination, loves dreaming and thinking, and the world of the fictional romantic heroes and heroines in the books she reads is just as significant to her as her everyday life.

5) Conscientiousness
Conscientious people are more methodical and likely to set a goal and stick to it. They are more reliable and work hard. They can easily motivate themselves to do a task they want to complete. They are tidier and organised, they think hard before they act and

they often have a strong sense of duty. People at the opposite end of the scale are more laid-back. They don't mind a bit of chaos, because they have different priorities in life. They are more likely to put unpleasant tasks off for another day.

I am always prepared
Very true...not at all true
I pay attention to details
Very true...not at all true
I like to get chores done promptly
Very true...not at all true
I hate poor organisation
Very true...not at all true
I have a schedule and stick to it
Very true...not at all true
My possessions are kept tidy
Very true...not at all true
I hate it if I don't fulfil my duties
Very true...not at all true

Crosses on the left show you lean towards conscientiousness. Edward's crosses would be strongly towards the left. He is tidy and has a strong sense of duty. His bedroom is immaculate and his CDs are organised by year and personal preference. He likes to do things the 'proper' way. Jacob's character is at the laid-back end of the spectrum. He is more spontaneous in the way he organises his life and is not particularly interested in his duties, such as being an active member of the Quileute pack.

These five personality factors are generally fixed traits that you will carry with you for your entire life. It is very difficult to change these aspects of yourself.

But there are a further aspects to your personality, which may be less fixed, for example your integrity, your self-esteem, your flexibility and your satisfaction with life.

Integrity
Integrity is to do with your 'moral compass'. Some people have unwavering morals and apply rules strictly. Others see rules as being more like guidelines, to be changed if the circumstances justify it.

I feel guilty whenever I tell a lie
Very true..not at all true
I hate to let friends down
Very true..not at all true
It is always wrong to deceive
Very true..not at all true
I could never forgive a cheat
Very true..not at all true
I do what's right, not what's easy
Very true..not at all true

Edward has a strong sense of right and wrong. Jacob is less strict in his attitude to morals – for example, he is happy to help Bella fix up two (strictly forbidden!) motorbikes, and to see her dip into her college fund to do it. If your marks are mostly to the left, then like Edward, you prefer to follow closely the rules for right and wrong. If you put marks on the right, then like Jacob, your moral judgements are more flexible and more likely to depend on the situation and viewpoint.

Self-esteem
How much value you put on yourself is part of your character, and extremely important in your relationships with men. In general,

if you have good self-esteem you will expect and are more likely to get good treatment from your boyfriend. You are more likely to feel sure of your partner's love for you and it will be easier to trust them.

What is your current self-esteem like?

I'm not comfortable with myself
Very true...not at all true
I don't think I'll be a success
Very true...not at all true
I'm disappointed with myself
Very true...not at all true
I don't like taking responsibility
Very true...not at all true
I am less capable than most people
Very true...not at all true
My life lacks direction
Very true...not at all true
I feel I can't deal with things
Very true...not at all true

The more your marks are to the right of the page, the higher your self-esteem is. If your marks are towards the left, don't immediately assume there's something wrong with you. It's not at all unusual – many young women feel low self-esteem.

And self-esteem can change; it can be improved with good life experiences and support. In a year's time your crosses might be in different places.

However, low self-esteem can become habit-forming. People become set in their ways, and this applies to self-esteem just as much as anything else. A lot of young women remain trapped like this, never valuing themselves enough. Persistent low self-esteem is a problem that needs to be addressed, so if you are concerned, seek some help.

Bella's experience is an illustration of how self-esteem can change. Her crosses on the scale above began at the left at the start of *Twilight*, then shifted across to the right by the end of *Breaking Dawn*.

Because of her relationships with Edward, Jacob and the rest of the Cullen clan, Bella gradually began to value herself more. The Cullens and Jacob gave her clear messages that she was important and valuable to them. She began to believe it. (And becoming a beautiful, immortal, super-strong vampire helped!)

Flexibility

Another important aspect to your personality is the way you deal with conflict. Because everyone is different, at some point you will come up against someone who sees things differently to you. How you react when there is a clash of ideas will affect your relationships.

I adjust without many problems
Very true..not at all true
I am good at taking advice
Very true..not at all true
I can handle criticism easily
Very true..not at all true
I am easy to satisfy
Very true..not at all true
I don't mind being contradicted
Very true..not at all true
Arguments don't bother me
Very true..not at all true
I never mind if plans are changed
Very true..not at all true

I'm not particularly sensitive
Very true...not at all true

If you are high on flexibility – crosses to the left – you will have an easier time getting along with others, including boyfriends. Arguments will quickly resolve and won't bother you unduly. If you are low on flexibility, you'll find yourself getting into more arguments – and those arguments will probably mean more to you.

As people go through life and mature they usually get better at dealing with conflict. We learn to deal with criticism and arguments, and can put minor problems into context.

Edward, Jacob and Bella weren't particularly flexible people at first. But conflict is at the heart of any good novel. The conflicts between Bella, Jacob, Edward and the rest of the vampires and werewolves are what make the story so exciting. People agreeing with each other and getting along doesn't work in fiction! Imagine if Bella said to Edward: 'I'll take your advice and won't get involved with you. You're saying you are dangerous and I believe it. How about you become my friend on Facebook and we'll leave it at that?'

Satisfaction with life
How satisfied you are with your life can influence a lot of your feelings and behaviour. If you are very satisfied with your life, you are more likely to be laid-back and generous to others. If you are very dissatisfied, you may be a more restless person and quicker to judge others.

I am satisfied with my life
Very true...not at all true
What I've achieved so far pleases me
Very true...not at all true

Most people feel dissatisfied with their work or studies at some point or other; for example, when a job feels like a dead end. And most people feel satisfied at some point in their life, such as when a new relationship is going well.

A feeling of chronic dissatisfaction can permeate your relationships. If you are totally unhappy with your life, you are more likely to be dissatisfied with your man.

But dissatisfaction doesn't have to be a negative thing. It can be a positive thing, in that it gives you energy to change things for the better. After all, what would life be like if our ancestors had been satisfied with a lifestyle based on the technology of knocking two bits of rock together?

Bella, Edward and Jacob were all dissatisfied with their lives in the story. But with a combination of true love, imprinting, vanquishing their enemies and becoming immortal their life satisfaction rating went up considerably.

THIS IS ALL WELL AND GOOD BUT...

These personality factors are important to know – they give you a fundamental understanding of who you are.

But personality measures can only tell you so much... Human beings are so sophisticated, varied and complicated that we can't possibly be summed up by paper and pen in a few questionnaires. There's much more to you than this. There's no complete system for explaining and describing you perfectly.

It can help, though, to take a closer look at your emotions. Psychologists have discovered that people are driven far more by feelings than intellect. Research shows that people make decisions based on emotions, not logic.

To understand yourself better it can help to look at the emotions that drive you most, both positive and negative.

YOUR SIX POSITIVE EMOTIONS

According to psychologist Paul Ekman, the main positive emotions are happiness, pride, amusement/pleasure, excitement, contentment and satisfaction. One way of understanding yourself is to gain an insight into how these emotions affect you. Everyone is different in the way these positive emotions shape them.

For example, one girl may be much more driven by the pride she feels in her studies than the pleasure she takes from food, so she may work long into the night and forget to eat. Another girl might knock off college early to catch the half-price all-you-can-eat buffet.

Let's explore your positive emotions. As before, there are no right or wrong answers, no good or bad. It's about finding out who you are, not about judging yourself. See if you can answer the questions below. It may help to write it down or talk about your answers with a close friend.

1) Happiness
Because *Twilight* is a romance, Bella, Edward and Jacob all sought happiness through finding love. What gives you happiness in life? Have a go at filling in the blanks:

The things that give me/will give me the greatest happiness in life are:...
....

2) Pride
Pride is the positive feeling you get from your achievements. What do you take great pride in, and how much does this drive you as a person?

I take most pride in:..
....

3) Amusement/pleasure

What gives you most enjoyment when you're out to have fun? And how important is it to you that you have these things in your life?

The things I enjoy most in life are:...
....

4) Contentment

What most gives you the feeling of relaxed well-being? Curling up with a good book or walking in the countryside? Do you make the time for relaxation and contentment?

The things that make me feel contented are:..............................
....

5) Satisfaction

What gives you the most satisfaction? For example, you might get great satisfaction from keeping your house clean and tidy, or keeping fit, or helping others.

I get most satisfaction from:...
....

6) Excitement

Some people seek excitement much more than others, and the type of thing that excites you says something about who you are. One girl might get excited by a new nightclub, while another might be excited by solving a quadratic equation. What excites you? How important is excitement in your life?

The things that excite me most are:..
....

YOUR SIX NEGATIVE EMOTIONS

As you know, life is not all about fun and happiness. Part of your make-up involves negative emotions. According to Paul Ekman, the main negative emotions are sadness, anger, fear, contempt, guilt, shame/embarrassment.

At the beginning of this chapter, you looked at how much you are prone to some of the negative emotions. Try answering the questions below to gain an understanding of what these negative emotions are about.

1) Contempt
Who do you look down on and why? Many people have strong negative feelings about certain types of people or behaviours.

The kind of behaviours I despise in others are:............................
....

2) Anger
What things make your blood boil?

I get really angry when:...
....

3) Sadness
What kind of things make you feel sad?

I get very sad about:..
....

4) Fear

Most people are scared of something. Bella was afraid of interacting with people. Edward was terrified of losing Bella. Jacob was afraid of losing his freedom because of his duties as a member of the Quileute pack. What are your greatest fears?

The things I fear most are:...
....

5) Guilt

Unnecessary guilt is a bad thing, but having some guilt shows you have consideration for others. Edward felt a huge amount of guilt because of his bloodthirsty urges. The amount of guilt he experienced showed that he cared for other people. What makes you feel guilty?

I feel guilty when:...
....

6) Shame/embarrassment

These negative feelings happen when we think others see how inadequate or inferior we are. Bella frequently felt embarrassed. This told us she was not confident at all about the way she came across to others. What makes you feel ashamed or embarrassed?

I feel ashamed/embarrassed about:...
....

Out of the six positive and six negative emotions above, which ones do you think drive you the most?

AND NOW THE MOST DELICATE TOPIC IN ADULT LOVING RELATIONSHIPS...

Money.

For people with romantic ideals, money is a dirty word. Many people feel true love should not be sullied by considerations of wealth. Bella was very disparaging about Catherine in *Wuthering Heights* for spurning Heathcliff. Heathcliff was a penniless gypsy boy so Catherine married the local landowner instead. This wasn't very romantic of her.

But, unromantic or not, money matters. Attitude toward money is a very important consideration when it comes to finding a long-term partner.

For most women, a man's earning potential is important. Have you ever seen scantily clad girls flock around a beggar on the street, trying to catch his eye? Or seen them hang around the bankruptcy courts, hoping to attract the newly destitute? No – they lurk around exclusive nightclubs hoping to meet a millionaire footballer. That's why I wouldn't write a book called, *'True Love, Abject Poverty and You: How to Find a Boyfriend Who Will Make You Homeless'*.

If you are like most women, you will naturally be attracted to guys who are wealthier or the same level as you, rather than ones much poorer than you. There is nothing wrong with this. Throughout the animal kingdom, females show preference for males who can offer them better resources. It's Mother Nature, don't fight it. You can't help it; any more than young men can help fancying young, pretty girls more than very old ladies.

Material pressures are a strong force, sometimes stronger than love. Couples argue about money more than almost anything else.

Financial problems are cited as one of the most common reasons why couples split up.

Like it or not, love and money can't be prised apart. This doesn't mean you need a millionaire to make you happy, but it does mean that you need to be on the same page as your boyfriend in terms of attitudes, feelings, expectations and behaviour where money is concerned.

Your true love is likely to be similar to you in this area. It's not very romantic, which is why you won't read a love story like this:

> *Juliet stood in the queue at the bank. She reached over to pick up the leaflet on personal equity plans at exactly the time as the handsome stranger next to her. She felt a jolt of electricity as their fingers touched. He gazed into her eyes and said, 'So you're interested in tax free savings too?'*
>
> *'Oh yes,' she said huskily. 'I already have an ISA and because I'm a higher-rate taxpayer I need to manage my savings in an optimal tax-efficient way.'*
>
> *The stranger crooked an eyebrow. 'That's fascinating. The name's Romeo, by the way.'*
>
> *As they talked, Juliet realised Romeo shared her passion for index-linked government saving certificates. When he mentioned his equity unit trusts she fell deeply in love and from that moment their destiny was entwined forever.*

Money isn't a foundation for love, but being compatible in this area is necessary. If you are careful with your cash and watch every penny, you won't be happy with a guy who throws money around like water. Tightwads and spendthrifts generally don't make happy couples. Or you may differ on the amount you need to be contented. Some people are happy with modest means. Others feel they have failed in life unless they earn more and more each year. Some people can sleep soundly at night owing thousands to the bank. Other people are awake all night if their savings account drops below five figures.

Your attitude to money

I spend money carelessly
Very true...not at all true
The money I have now satisfies me
Very true...not at all true
Better a good life than a big salary
Very true...not at all true
The future will take care of itself
Very true...not at all true
I happily give money to others
Very true...not at all true

Understanding your thoughts on money is important. How much money is enough for you? What do you love – and hate – to spend money on? Your spending habits can point to where your priorities lie in life and help to reveal the kind of person you are. If your marks are more to the left, then, like Bella, money is not an important driving factor for you. If your crosses are to the right, then you take money much more seriously.

Be honest with yourself. Again, there is no right or wrong answer. Don't criticise yourself for how you genuinely feel. Some people feel money is very important, others don't care all that much. Such is the variation in human personality.

MORE ABOUT YOU

Money is not the only 'non-romantic' subject that matters in a relationship. Do any of the following ten areas stand out in your mind as a central part of who you are?

1) Education: how important is education to you? What level of education have you had/are planning to have?

2) Work: where does work fit into your life? Does it matter a great deal to you – are you extremely hardworking? Or is it just something to pay the rent?

3) Politics: are you passionate about some political view or other? Or not interested?

4) Spirituality: does religion or spirituality play a big part in your life?

5) Leisure: how do you like to spend your leisure time? What do you hate doing in your leisure time?

6) Social class/economic background: would you describe yourself as coming from a working-, middle-, or upper-class background? Does it even matter to you? How has your economic background shaped your tastes, expectations, attitudes in life?

7) Social life: is this a central part of your life? The type of person you are is partly defined by the friendships you have. Bella didn't have any friends, which tells us something important about her. What type of social life do you have and what does this say about you?

8) Passions: do you have any passions which are so strong they almost define who you are? For example, imagine someone who is so passionate about swimming that they go on to win an Olympic medal. They will be known as 'the Olympic gold medallist for swimming' for the rest of their lives. Are there any things in life that are so important to you, that if they were taken away, you almost wouldn't know who you are?

9) Health: what are your views and behaviours with regard to smoking, diet, exercise, alcohol and drugs?

10) Activity/energy level: are you a laid-back, stay-at-home type of person? Or do you hate to be stuck inside watching TV and would rather be very active?

For several of these ten questions you probably don't care much either way. For example, you might have no interest in politics or have a flexible attitude towards spirituality. But the areas that are important to you need taking into account when thinking about the type of boyfriend you need.

Some of these aspects of life might change over time. Maybe you're not too interested in work now, at this stage of your life, but see yourself pushing forward towards career success in the future. Or perhaps you enjoy a lifestyle of going out and partying now, but picture yourself staying at home with a family of your own one day. This brings us to another important aspect of yourself: your goals in life.

YOUR GOALS

To a large extent you can't judge a person by where they are now. You have to look at where they are going.

For example, imagine two identical twin girls called Sophie and Alexia, both smart and attractive. Both have just started studying law at university.

But they are heading in different directions. Sophie's dream is to get a first in her degree and plans to work in a top City firm, before setting up her own practice.

Alexia wants to drop out as soon as her next student loan comes through the post. She plans to use the money to buy a train ticket to Wales where she'll live in a yurt at an eco commune.

They are both perfectly legitimate plans. Happiness can be achieved by either path. But their plans reveal their very different characters.

Some couples fall in love before realising their goals are completely incompatible. If one person is desperate to move to the country and live in a smallholding and the other has a life dream to go and live in Manhattan, it may not work.

Although this may be early days for you, this includes goals about children. If you dream of having babies one day and your boyfriend is adamant he never will, it's not going to work long term.

What are your goals in life?

Some people don't have any particular plans, they live day to day. They enjoy the moment, see how life unfolds. They don't see life as marching towards a goal. This is fine; there is no right or wrong way to be. But your view of the future needs to be compatible with your boyfriend's. Wanting the same things can bind you together – wanting different things can lead you to grow apart.

Maybe you don't know what your goals are. But do you know what you *don't* want? What's your worst nightmare? To be stuck in your current life, which you find dissatisfying? Or to be forced to move somewhere new, to change what is dearly loved and familiar?

Think, write or talk with a friend about the following three things:

1) These are my wildest dreams for the future:
2) This is my worst nightmare for the future:
3) These are my realistic hopes for the future:

EXERCISES TO INCREASE YOUR SELF-AWARENESS

I hope this chapter has given you a deeper insight into who you are. To develop further, try the following six exercises.

1) Keep a secret diary

Get a diary with a lock and keep it in a safe place. Write in your diary every day, or as often as you can. Write down anything you like – how you feel about what happened that day, your observations, your view about the events in your day-to-day life.

Write about your secret hates, wishes, dreams, fantasies. You can put down what you like – no one will see it but you.

Then, after a few weeks, go back and read what you have written. Ask yourself, as if you were a stranger reading the diary for the first time, who is this girl? What can you learn from the private thoughts and feelings? What drives this person? What did you write about? What does this say about you? What are your vulnerabilities? What are your strengths?

2) Consider what you would like to change about yourself

Think or write about who you would like to be, if you could transform into your ideal self. Look at what you'd like to change about yourself. What does this tell you about your values or priorities?

3) Write about your deepest feelings

Get a pad of paper out and just start writing about your deepest feelings – the most emotional experience of your life. Don't edit what you are going to say. Just write anything that comes to mind. Look back at your writing later. What can you learn about yourself from what you have written?

4) Look at what people say about you (good and bad)

What have you been told about yourself by other people? If you have heard the same criticism about yourself from different people, then it's likely there's a grain in truth in what they say. It doesn't mean you are a bad person – nobody's perfect! Is there some truth in the criticism? What useful feedback about yourself was in the criticism? They are reacting to something in you. What could it be?

Bella had lots of negative reactions from Jessica. Part of this was jealousy, because Bella was getting a lot of attention from the guys. But part of it was probably Bella's aloofness. When Bella first met Jessica, Bella didn't really try to interact with her. She wasn't interested in Jessica at all, and didn't bother to even try to follow her conversation for politeness' sake. The only questions Bella asked Jessica was a series of questions about the Cullens. This is not how you should interact with someone who has taken the trouble to talk to you on your first day in a new school. You need to make an effort to be interested; after all, you are trying to establish yourself in a new social group. Bella was only interested in the beautiful people.

Jessica's negative reaction to Bella, although perhaps unfair, said something about Bella. It spoke volumes about Bella's social skills.

5) Think about the people you can't stand

Write down a list of people who you really dislike. Write down what it is about them that gets under your skin. Try to identify the qualities you detest.

Now you have identified what it is about them you don't like, look at what this says about you. Your strong reaction says something. It's usually the case that you are the exact opposite to them on that quality. For example, Bella really didn't like Jessica. She couldn't abide Jessica's giggling and gossipy conversation. This tells us that Bella is seriously minded and not that interested in others (unless they have fangs or shape-shifting abilities, of course).

But sometimes, the qualities you can't stand in others are ones you don't like in yourself.

6) Think about the people who inspire you

Do you identify with any particular characters in books, films or on TV? They could be real or fictional. Talk about your feelings with a friend. What is it about them that inspires you? Bella identified strongly with heroines of classic romantic fiction.

This tells us she was hungry for romance herself. And that she identified most strongly with fictional characters in long-dead worlds perhaps gives us a clue that she did not feel she belonged in the world she lived in.

YOUR CONCLUSIONS

Understanding yourself better is the foundation of finding love and a satisfying relationship with a man. Understanding men will get you nowhere if you don't first understand yourself.

But first, recap on what are the most important things about you. Ask a friend to help – you could help them come up with their own list. Include your strengths, your values, your weaknesses, your vulnerabilities.

For example, Bella might have come up with some of the following important aspects of herself:

- Her imaginative intellect.
- She is lonely.
- She loves reading.
- She is not at all interested in money.
- She is prone to feeling anxious with people.
- She is an introvert.
- She dislikes socialising and has difficulties making friends.
- She's not that interested in people.
- She's not particularly satisfied with her life.
- Her self-esteem is low.
- She gets great satisfaction from helping others while sacrificing herself.

Now write down your own list.

WHAT DO THESE ANSWERS MEAN FOR FUTURE RELATIONSHIPS WITH MEN?

Bella might have answered:

I need a guy who...

- Has an appreciation of imagination and literature.
- Likes a quiet social life.
- Is sensitive, supportive and understanding.
- Isn't going to take advantage of my drive to sacrifice myself for others.

I should not get involved with a guy who...

- Is keen on socialising.
- Thinks reading and imagination is a waste of time.
- Sees life as being about acquiring wealth.
- Is impatient with people who are nervous or lacking confidence.
- Will exploit my giving and self-sacrificing nature.
- Wants to kill me (this should be on every girls list!).

Now write your own lists.

SECRET STEP FOUR: SUMMARY

The secret of knowing yourself is:

- Understanding how your past relationships have shaped who you are.
- Recognising and dealing with your personal baggage.
- Understanding your personality traits and emotions.
- Knowing your own goals in life.
- Knowing where you stand on the things in life that are important to you.

Now it's time to look at men...

SECRET FIVE

How to Get a Deep Insight Into Your Boyfriend

(Uncover the truth about who your man really is)

CHAPTER 13

WHY THE TRUTH ABOUT A MAN IS HARD TO SEE

Bella could see the truth about Edward and Jacob. She could tell that they were both good people, despite the fact that Edward was a vampire and Jacob a werewolf. When you read or watched *Twilight*, you made the same judgments as Bella. In fiction it is usually easy to spot the heroes – and the villains. In our own lives, it's not always quite so easy...

Are you a good judge of other people? You'll probably say yes. And it's true, that as a woman you are better judge of character than men. Studies show women pay attention to others and listen more, so are better at picking up clues about a person.

BUT, when it comes to judging an attractive man, these good instincts and superior powers of observation often seem to pack up their bags and go home.

WHY WOMEN DON'T LISTEN

Why do women have difficulty in paying attention to information about an attractive man? Simple: when you are with a man you fancy, you are more likely to be self-conscious.

In other words, the focus of your attention is inwards – on you. You are paying attention to a whole load of information that's going on inside yourself. You are concerned about how you are coming across.

Psychology studies have found that when people focus attention on themselves, they are not as good at judging other people. They miss vital information about the person to whom they are talking.

When you are focusing on what he thinks of you, you are not paying enough attention to what you think of him. You miss important signs about his personality.

WHY IT'S EASY TO MISJUDGE A MAN

Sometimes you can look at something right in front of your nose, but not see it. It's not just when you are judging men, it happens all the time. For example, 'looked but didn't see' is one of the most common causes of traffic accidents. People look but don't see the hazard that leads to a crash.

Why is this? It's because of inattentiveness.

For example, what colour is the writing on the front of this book? The chances are you didn't notice. You won't see something unless you deliberately look for it.

WHY YOU CAN'T SPOT THE GORILLA

There is a clever test of attention where you are asked to watch a video clip of a basketball game. Take a look if you haven't seen it – search for 'basketball attention test' on YouTube. You are told to count how many passes the players in white make and you watch carefully for 30 seconds. Nothing particular happens, you count the passes and you get the number right. It's just an ordinary game of basketball.

Then, you are shown the same clip again and told to look for a gorilla. This time, you see there is a man dressed in a gorilla costume, walking in clear view among the players. Despite the fact your eyes were on the screen and the gorilla was in full view the first time you watched the clip, you probably didn't notice it. Most people don't.

If you are focusing on something hard, you can miss something else that's right in front of you. The reason for this is your brain can only process so much information at a time. Your brain is like a computer and it would crash if it tried to handle all the information coming in from all of your senses. So even though your eyes are getting information about something, the brain will ignore it. What you don't pay attention to, you won't see.

When you meet a new man, a huge amount of information about him is available to you – often before you have even met him. He is telling you a thousand things about himself before you even hear him speak. Much of this is missed because we don't see it. There may be something very important about him, but you are oblivious. It is easy to miss the gorilla. I will talk about how to overcome this problem in the next chapter, but lack of attention is not the only problem...

HIS COURTSHIP DISPLAY

Another difficulty in judging men is that in the first few weeks of your relationship, you may not see the real him. You'll see him performing his courtship display. This may – or may not – bear much resemblance to the person he is inside.

Men usually have to make an effort to attract a woman. They have to convince you they would be a good prospect. Like the peacock that spreads its beautiful tail, the guy will try to present himself in the best possible light. He will show you aspects of himself he thinks you'll be impressed by. So men will display a range of behaviour in the hope you'll be beguiled. This could include boasting about his achievements, a macho display of strength and dominance, a display of his sensitivity and thoughtfulness, hints about his fascinating nature, showering you with gifts, raining compliments on your head, demonstrations of his incredible intelligence, his wit or whatever else he thinks will get you hooked.

It's nice to be courted in this way. But the trouble with this courtship behaviour is that it may not represent fundamental parts of his personality. The display of sensitivity and thoughtfulness may become much less in evidence once you are a couple, and you may even discover he is usually thoughtless and selfish.

To illustrate this point here is an imaginary case study of a peahen that falls in love with a peacock because of his tail:

Patricia was a young peahen looking for her dream peacock. She met Darren lazing under an elm tree.

'He sprang to his feet and immediately displayed his tail. It was dazzling. The way the colours shimmered, the glossiness of the feathers, the sheer size. I was mesmerised, I don't mind admitting.'

Patricia became his mate without much further thought. 'We spent hours of bliss together. He'd wave his tail in front of me, I'd practically swoon, and we'd sneak off into the bushes together. It wasn't long before I had a clutch of eggs in the nest.'

It was then that the problems started. Darren gradually stopped bothering with his tail display and spent his time lazing about. He didn't see the point; they were a couple now. 'I felt disappointed,' Patricia admitted. 'I looked at him with his tail down and saw he was nothing special. Quite plain-looking, really. I challenged him, asked him why he didn't spread his tail out like he used to. He said, "Look, it really tires me out to lift that thing up. And it's a damn nuisance the way it keeps catching on everything." He gave me an accusing look over his beak. "Anyway, you should love the bird underneath, not the tail." We had our first row and I was left crying bitterly.'

But she realised the truth. 'He was right. I didn't love the bird underneath. I loved his tail feathers.'

They split up and Patricia was left to bring up her brood alone. She is now dating a pheasant.

Like the peacock's tail, your man's courtship behaviour may not bear much relationship to the real man underneath. A man can revert to his true character after he feels it's no longer necessary to put on a courtship display. This is why girls often say, 'I don't understand it... he was really nice in the beginning.' The reason is, he has stopped bothering to spread out his tail feathers.

You can't judge a man until you see him in his normal mode of behaviour. It's not a good idea to love a peacock because of his tail. When this happens with humans it's not such a laughing matter, though. This is the story of one couple I spoke to:

Twenty-four-year-old Cheryl was excited when her new boyfriend, Scott, picked her up for a date. His sports car roared into her parents' cul-de-sac, causing much net curtain twitching. Cheryl didn't know much about cars, but she knew that Scott's car, low-slung, a two-seater and sleek, was an expensive make. She was impressed when Scott took her to the opening night of a new celebrity-chef-owned restaurant. There were TV cameras, free champagne and paparazzi as well as food to die for. Cheryl looked forward to each date. They always went somewhere exciting, like a top-end nightclub, full of models and footballers. Scott didn't seem to mind paying the eye-watering prices at these places that she certainly couldn't afford on her salary as an HR assistant. As their relationship developed, the big nights happened less often; instead, Scott would cook her a meal at his flat. Although

Cheryl was a foodie like Scott, she hankered after a bit of excitement, too.

That's why she suggested they go away for the weekend in Paris. She googled some top restaurants, nightclubs and hotels and talked to Scott. He said, 'I'd love to go. Just one thing, can you pay for us both this time? I haven't got much money this month. I'll pay for the next one.'

Cheryl's excitement drained away a little. The thought of spending her own money on him wasn't quite so enticing. 'I don't think I've got enough money for us both.'

'But nor do I,' said Scott.

Cheryl felt embarrassed and irritated, 'But you used to throw quite a lot of cash around.'

Scott raised an eyebrow. 'I know, but I was trying to impress you, I thought you were special. I couldn't help it. I shouldn't have really; I spent all of my bonus. I have to live a bit more quietly now. Hey, are you pouting?' he said, putting his arms around her. 'We don't have to have money to have a good time – we're in love, aren't we?'

Cheryl frowned and pulled away. 'You say you want to live quietly, but you're happy enough to spend all that money on a car.'

'Not any more. Cheryl, to tell you the truth, I can't afford it, not really. My car's on a lease, I don't own it. It costs almost as much as my rent. I've been wondering why I spend so much on it. And to be honest, the main reason is it impresses the girls. And I don't need to do that any more. I've got you. I'm going to get rid of it at the end of the month and get something more run of the mill.'

'You're getting rid of your car?' said Cheryl.

'Why are you looking at me like that?' he said. 'Does that bother you – you think less of me?'

'No,' said Cheryl quickly. 'Of course I don't.' But her face betrayed that she was lying. She did think less of him. She knew it, and he knew it.

She ended the relationship soon after.

Scott was broken-hearted. It took him months to get over her. He stopped enjoying things, even went off his food. He slowly realised that Cheryl had been beguiled by his courtship strategy, rather than him as a person.

He can now talk about it without getting too upset. 'The trouble with Cheryl,' he smiles wryly, 'is that she liked the sizzle, not the sausage.'

THE POWER DYNAMICS

Typically in male–female relationships, girls find it relatively easy to attract prospective partners, whereas men have to work harder to please the choosy female. In the early days, you are deciding whether or not to reject him. You are far more likely to reject his sexual advances than he is to reject yours. A study was conducted where men and women were tasked with chatting up a stranger of the opposite sex and asking if they'd like to go to bed with them. Seventy-five per cent of the men approached said yes. None of the women did.

The fact that he's chasing you gives you the upper hand at first. You are the one deciding whether or not to reject him. In other words, you have more power.

Power dynamics affect people's behaviour. How you behave towards your boss's boss is completely different to how you'd behave towards a homeless man on the street. You are unlikely to hang on to the homeless guy's every word and laugh loudly at his jokes. Your boss's boss has the power to make your life difficult – or reward you. With a powerful person, you will listen carefully to what they say, show deference and respect, and go out of your way to please.

This applies to your man, too. How a man behaves when he is with someone who has more power than him is completely different to how he behaves towards someone with less power. So, while you are holding all the cards and are deciding whether or not to reject him, he will naturally be more respectful, eager to please and accommodating. This may change once he feels confident you won't reject him.

This is how bullies get girlfriends. They don't bully her on the first date (as a rule – but I have heard this happen!). They are considerate, reasonable, nice. They know that they won't get a girl if they are pushy or unpleasant. They naturally behave themselves.

Thankfully, the majority of men are not bullies, and wouldn't dream of hurting you. But the way he behaves to you in the early days isn't necessarily his true personality. It may be that he is behaving in a much nicer way than usual.

HE CREATES A ROMANCE ABOUT HIMSELF

By creating 'a romance', I mean in the old-fashioned sense – romance as in an 'improbable story'. When it comes to relationships, all too often women fall in love with a fiction they have woven around their man. But sometimes it's not you creating the illusions. It's him...

Georgina, an 18-year-old psychology student, met Evan through her university friends.

Evan was 27 and an artist. Although Evan had talent, he didn't want to make a living from it. He was an artist who didn't expect to be paid – and didn't want to be paid.

'He told me he despised the commercial world. He called it a degrading ritual of grubbing for money. He made sculptures out of driftwood on the beach or discarded items in skips. He would spend days creating a piece, and

197

then give it away or dismantle it. He said it didn't matter if it didn't last. His favourite word was "transient". Art always had to be "transient".'

Evan told Georgina he was a loner and the world didn't understand him. He presented himself as someone in a world that refused to accept him for who he was. He couldn't accept the conventional rules of society. Evan opened Georgina's eyes to a different world view.

'I was from a very conventional background, where people worked hard at their studies and got a job. He didn't care about material values. He wasn't like anyone else I'd ever met and I was fascinated. He was a rebel in society, refusing to be cut into the mould of the worker. He said he hadn't many girlfriends because he was extremely choosy. He thought love was precious, to be shared with someone special. I was that special person.'

Georgina saw him as a romantic figure and, dazzled, she fell in love.

But his story obscured some facts which were at odds with his image of himself. The first was that although Evan despised the material world, and the society which tried to mould him, he didn't despise it enough to refuse handouts. Georgina discovered later that for years he'd existed on a combination of benefits and 'loans' from his hardworking mother. He didn't want to enter the commercial world of sculpture because deep down he was terrified of failure.

'It took me one month to fall in love with him, but a year to untangle the story of who he really was. He was a loner because most of the people he knew had moved on with their lives, leaving him still hanging around with university students much younger than him. And

I found out he had once had a conventional job as an artist working for the council but had got himself sacked. Part of his contempt for the working world was because it rejected him. For months he was vague about the details – till I finally heard he'd done a project with a class of fourteen-year-olds, helping them create a garden sculpture in the school, but had been sacked for passing round a marijuana joint for them to try.'

Georgina discovered why he'd had few serious girlfriends. It wasn't because he was choosy, or waiting for someone special. It was because few girls wanted to get serious with him once they found out his life plan was to stay on benefits until he could draw his pension.

'My friends kept telling me he was a loser. But I was convinced I'd found the love of my life. The thing is, Evan genuinely believes in his own self-image. He would pass a lie detector test without sweat. I thought I knew him, but all I knew was the illusion he believed in.'

THE INTIMACY CIRCLE

There's another reason why it's hard to find out the truth about a man. It's because when you first meet him he will obey the unwritten rules about how to behave when meeting someone you don't know.

With a stranger, people tend to be polite and cautious. At first you stick to easy topics like the weather, or a remark about your surroundings. You will keep your distance. You will treat each other with respect. You'll move on to basic topics like where you live, or your jobs. You'll try to find common ground. Everyone knows these conventions.

There are different rules of behaviour depending on how well you know a person. The more intimately you know a person, the more the rules change. The diagram below shows the pattern of intimacy for most people.

On the outside of your circle there are casual acquaintances; the postman, the people you nod or say hello to at a gym class or a local shop. The rules are to stick to small talk.

In the next circle are your casual friends, or friends of friends. They are not a central part of your life. You don't reveal much of yourself to them.

The next layer of closeness might be the friends you go out and have fun with, or your work colleagues. You wouldn't ring them up first in a crisis, or tell them all your personal problems. Similarly, you don't know everything that's going on in their lives.

The closest person to you may be a boyfriend, parent or best friend. You can be yourself with them, you can show your true colours, reveal most of your real thoughts and emotions – and so can they.

You know yourself best. There may be things about yourself that you haven't shared with anyone. On your own you can indulge in socially unacceptable or forbidden behaviour.

You can't tell what a person is really like if they are not in your inner circle. You can't learn much about a person through small talk or casual talk. This is why people are always surprised when they hear about a crime committed by a casual acquaintance. 'But he seemed so normal,' they say. That's because people follow the normal rules of polite conversation when in public view.

So when you first meet a man, he will probably obey the rules of behaviour for a stranger meeting a stranger. It's not really possible to judge how he behaves in an intimate relationship. You've little idea how he would treat a regular girlfriend.

As you get to know him better, you will pass through the levels of intimacy and each stage will reveal more about the real him.

But the problem is, many girls judge a man by his behaviour on that initial meeting. 'He was really nice!' they'll gush. But I am afraid you can't really tell if someone is nice or not, when you are at this very surface level of intimacy. He may be charming with strangers, but not very nice to his girlfriends. You don't know what he does on his own. He might not be nice at all!

KEEP YOUR MIND OPEN

People often stick with a first impression. Once you've made your judgement of someone, it's not easy to change your opinion.

When Bella first met Jacob, she judged him as being a kind, harmless, easy-going, straightforward person. This was the person she called 'my Jacob'. But once Jacob became a shape-shifter, he fundamentally changed. He couldn't carry on being the happy-go-lucky young man. He kept turning into a ravening werewolf. He had a responsibility to the Quileute tribe. He had to think about ridding his territory of marauding vampires. He became moody, difficult and dangerous. This was the truth about who he became. Yet Bella kept on insisting he was still 'her Jacob', that the old Jacob remained somewhere inside him. But he was no longer this person.

DELIBERATE DECEPTION

Men lie. And women do, of course. It's very common for males and females to lie to each other in the dating game. This can go from mild deception to whopping great fibs. Humans are no different to the rest of the animal kingdom, who often use deception to get a mate.

Men and women tend to lie about different things. Women use more deception about their appearance. You might employ trickery of a mild kind – such as hair extensions or a padded bra, or wearing control pants so you appear to have the ideal hip-to-waist ratio that men prefer. Older women lie about their age, or spend thousands on anti-ageing procedures. Another common deception is to conceal how many boyfriends you've had.

A man is more likely to lie about his income and power in society. Or he may lie about his intentions towards you. He may want short-term fun, but fake an interest in long-term investment.

REAL MEN ARE MORE COMPLICATED THAN WEREWOLVES AND VAMPIRES

In some ways, Bella had an easier time in finding out the truth about Edward and Jacob's characters. They were easier to understand than real-life humans.

The most important thing she needed to know about Edward was that he was a vampire. The other thing that defined him was his love for Bella. He had very little existence outside Bella. That he loved her deeply and wanted to protect her drove all of his behaviours. There was little more she needed to know to understand him.

Similarly, the most important thing to understand about Jacob was that he was werewolf, whose existence entailed a hatred of vampires. This shaped most of his behaviours – plus, of course, his passion for Bella.

It's not quite as straightforward as this in real life.

The human male has a whole range of thoughts, feelings, wishes, dreams, hates, interests, passions and habits that have nothing do with you. He has had a complete existence without you in it, and even if you stay together forever will he continue to have whole parts of him that are not centred on you.

He will be contradictory. Lots of aspects of him will not fit together easily. He will surprise and perhaps disappoint you. You may think you understand him one minute, then he will puzzle you the next. And the same applies to you, too. You have a whole existence outside your man, and you will surprise him.

But this isn't a problem. Getting to know each other's complexities is one of the fascinating things about having a healthy, adult relationship.

YOU MAY BE DISHEARTENED...

You may be thinking, how an earth can you judge a man, with all these pitfalls? It's not an easy task. This is why relationships can be painful. You have a relatively short window with a man before you may 'imprint' on him. And once you fall in love, you're even less likely to see the real him. So what can you do?

You can turn to the next chapter.

CHAPTER 14

HOW TO BE A GOOD JUDGE OF MEN

If we all had telepathic powers like Edward, judging other people would be a breeze. Edward can just look inside other people's heads and see what they are feeling and thinking. He can tell that Jessica, Bella's schoolmate, is shallow and spiteful. He knows that Charlie is a good man. But sadly, none of us have this gift. However, there are other ways to figure people out.

The key to being a great judge of men is:

Pay attention!

It sounds simple, but it's true. Bella pointed this out in *New Moon*. She told Jacob how good he was at reading her feelings and thoughts, despite the fact he didn't have telepathic powers. She said it was because he paid attention.

You can't see anything properly unless you are looking at it fully. You may remember the old Indian story of the blind men and the elephant:

> Four blind men heard there was an elephant in the village. They'd never heard of such a creature before, so they went to find out what it was like.
>
> One of them reached out his hand and felt the elephant's tail. He said, 'An elephant is like a piece of rope.'
>
> The second man touched the elephant's side. 'No, an elephant is like a wall.'

The third man reached out, found the ear and said, 'I think an elephant is like a fan.'

The fourth man felt the elephant's trunk. 'An elephant is like a branch of a tree.'

Each man formed a different opinion of the elephant because they only paid attention to part of it. They all missed vital information about the true nature of an elephant.

And it's easy to make the same mistake when judging a man. If you fail to pay attention to the whole person, you'll miss important aspects of who he is. Beware of reaching out and only touching his trunk!

To judge him properly you need to look at a whole lot more – and there are many different sources of information about a guy.

UNDERSTAND THE RELEVANCE OF GOSSIP

Bella learned something about Edward before she even spoke to him. She heard from Jessica and Mike that Edward didn't mix with anyone apart from his family and had earned himself a reputation for being 'weird'.

This gossip was pretty accurate. He did set himself apart from the others and there was something weird about him – he was a vampire!

A person's reputation is often well-earned and is worth careful attention.

Have you ever heard someone say proudly, 'I don't listen to gossip'? If it's true, they could be making a big mistake. Gossip plays a huge part in human life. Gossip, or exchanging personal information about each other, actually fulfils a very useful function.

For example, imagine you've just spent a pleasant morning gossiping with your workmate about whether your boss is pregnant. You've both noticed she keeps running to the loo, drank orange juice on the work night out and was cagey about making plans for the next year.

This is not just nosiness or idle chat. Whether she's pregnant is important information, which could have implications for your social position. Will you – or your workmate – take her job when she's on maternity leave? Should you start making sure she notices the good work you've been doing? Will the pregnancy make her cranky, and should you be more careful than usual about what you say?

Social lives are based on cooperation and trust. But some people take advantage of this and will take without giving. Never buying a round at the pub is an example of this behaviour. Gossip is vital for helping you spot these 'cheats'. If you've heard on the grapevine someone is untrustworthy, you can make sure you don't get taken for a ride.

Of course, it needs to be borne in mind that sometimes people get an undeserved reputation, because someone with a grudge is spreading false information about them. However, this happens less often than you might think. Psychology studies have shown that over 90 per cent of gossip is true, and not malicious fabrication.

✳ GOSSIP ✳

Everybody does it. Whether you are in a university common room full of grey-haired professors or a school canteen full of teenagers, the chances are that much of the conversation will be social chat. Studies show that whatever the setting, 60 to 70 per cent of all normal conversation is gossip.

It's seen as a female thing and men don't view themselves as gossips. But research has shown that men gossip just as much as women. However, their social chat has more of a 'boasting' flavour to it.

Perhaps surprisingly, only 5 per cent of gossip is negative in tone. And a huge 80 per cent of information in a typical tabloid newspaper is gossip.

A psychologist called Professor Robin Dunbar even has the theory that our brains became large in order to cope with the vast quantities of social information we need to process. So next time you are having a good gossip instead of working or studying, don't feel bad. You're fulfilling a vital social function and giving your brain a good workout at the same time!

Gossip about your man can give you an insight into how he has behaved in a range of situations with a number of people. It reveals clues about how he relates to other human beings. And because past behaviour predicts future behaviour, you can expect him to continue in the same pattern.

If a man has a reputation for some kind of negative behaviour, there is a good chance it's true, and there is a good chance he will repeat this behaviour.

So the first thing you need to do when you meet a new man, is to gather as much gossip as you can about him, and listen to it carefully. If he has a reputation for lying, womanising, cheating, gambling, aggression – or anything else you don't want in the love of your life – then don't go there. If you decide to ignore this information, then this is your choice, but it is at your own risk.

LOVE IN THE INFORMATION AGE

In the old days, it was a simple matter of meeting him face to face and falling in love. With modern technology, there are new ways to get to know a man, with a new set of pitfalls and dilemmas...

Should you google him?

There may be a wealth of information about your man at your fingertips. Using the Internet, you can access the electoral roll and find out who lives with him, use an ancestry website to trace his family, get information about his business from LinkedIn or read his blog. You could see his holiday snaps on Flickr, look at his social networking sites, see pictures of him other people have put on their sites, read an essay he wrote at college, see if he's taken part in any sponsored events, or signed online petitions.

In the past, only by hiring a private detective could you get information like this. One woman in New York googled her date and found out he was wanted by the FBI for stealing a hundred thousand dollars. She tipped off the police, who gave her date a nasty surprise when they turned up at the restaurant instead of her!

There is no accepted etiquette about googling yet. Do you google and then pretend you don't already know when he says he's done a sponsored trek up Kilimanjaro? Or do you admit to looking him up on the Internet and risk coming across as a bit creepy and stalker-ish? A survey in America showed 43 per cent of people admit googling their date. Whether you do or do not is a personal decision.

The pitfalls of social networking sites

What can you learn about a man from social networking sites like Facebook? If you haven't met him before, then the answer is: nothing!

If you only know a man from a social networking site, basically he's a stranger. Looking at the information on his pages cannot tell you anything about him. They are just images and words. They may not bear any relation to the person who wrote them.

Sadly, more than one girl has been killed by a sexual predator who used social networking sites to create fake profiles. So, unless you know him personally, every man who sends you a message or friend request is a stranger. Even if a friend of a friend contacts you, you still don't know who they are. Your own Facebook friend may have added them without knowing them personally.

A man you meet on Facebook, MySpace or Bebo is more of an unknown quantity than a stranger you bump into in real life. When you meet a complete stranger, at least you can tell roughly what age he is and what he looks like.

The safety advice for under-18s is to never meet up with anyone you only know online. If you are over 18, then meet up in a public place, plus preferably have someone with you or if not, at least tell someone where you are going.

Despite these dangers, a recent survey found 45 per cent of people thought social networking sites like Facebook were a good way of meeting the opposite sex, and thought it was more acceptable to meet a partner this way than dating websites. The same survey showed one in four people had dated someone they met though a social networking site.

Are social networking sites a good way of meeting men? There are anecdotal reports of people finding their soulmate this way. But it's too early to know for sure.

Another pitfall of social networking sites is that you get a false sense of intimacy. People know things about you because of the information on your page, so it feels like they're closer friends than they actually are.

For example, they may know what religion you follow, whereas in real life you probably wouldn't reveal this information before you'd got to know someone. A man can approach you with something personal, such as 'I see you're passionate about the environment', and start a conversation. It feels as if you've started chatting to a friend of a friend at a party.

In addition, because you are not face to face you are more likely to open up. Sitting at a computer miles away from someone means it doesn't feel as risky to reveal who you are. In a real-life social situation, you have to face the consequences of saying too much – you risk public rejection or embarrassment. Interacting online isn't like this as you can easily end the conversation any time you like.

How much can you read into his Facebook or computer dating information?

Even if the things he writes about himself are true, you can only get a very partial view of who he is as a person. Information online is a highly edited version of the man.

The problem is, our brains are very good at 'filling in the gaps' of our knowledge with a picture of who they may be.

For example – read this profile:

Basic info: male, blue eyes, dark hair, Taurus, non-smoker. Although I'm not a vegetarian, I try not to eat too much meat – I think a veggie diet is the healthiest.

Bio: the education system and I didn't see eye to eye – I was a bit of a rebel at school and left early. I love art and wanted to do it for a living, but this wasn't practical. I thought about being an architect for a while and then settled on going into politics. I am interested in animal rights and the environment. I believe more trees should be planted in the countryside and want reforms on animal protection.

My personality: I would describe myself as very ambitious and passionate about what I do. I always fight for what I believe in.

Interests: to relax, the thing I like to do best is to walk my dog, Blondi. I love old films, like Charlie Chaplin movies. When I can get away from work I go to my private retreat in the mountains.

How does he sound? What kind of image have you formed of this man? Might you be interested in seeing his picture? Everything in his profile is true.

The person in the profile is Adolf Hitler.

If you have some sketchy information about a man, like the information you get online, your imagination can fill in the gaps and create an image in your head. You might then fall in love with the image, not the real person. In a survey of online daters, 11 per cent of people said they fell in love with their partner before they'd even met.

Courtships seem to be quicker when a couple meet via a dating website. The average length before marriage is 18 months rather than the usual average of 42 months. Is this because computer technology has helped them find their perfect match? Or is it because people who use dating websites are at a stage in their life where they are ready to commit? Or is it that having information on a computer causes them make up their minds more quickly? We don't know the answers yet to these questions. And it's too early to say whether computer dating relationships are more or less successful than those where couples meet naturally.

Instant messaging

Getting to know a man through instant messaging has some pitfalls to bear in mind.

Even though you're interacting, he's not there in front of you. This gives your imagination free rein. Writing words on a keyboard is different from talking face to face. With the written word you receive no tone of voice, eye contact, facial expression or body language. All this important information is missing. Without it you can imagine a picture of him which is far removed from reality.

When writing down sentences there's much more time to edit. The words take longer to travel from his brain to his fingers, he has more time to think, and his words may be transformed on the way down. In real conversation, he will not talk this way. Face-to-face conversation gives more accurate information about a man. His spontaneous speech and slip-ups will reveal much more about his personality.

HOW YOU MEET

The way you meet a man reveals things about whether there is a chance of forming a serious, committed relationship with him.

The best chance of finding love is through people you know personally. Most long-term, loving relationships are found through people you know, via school, work, family, friends or your real-life social network (not social networking sites).

A survey carried out by Match.com of recently married couples found that 38 per cent met through work or school, 27 per cent through friends, 17 per cent on websites, 8 per cent in clubs and bars, and 4 per cent through churches.

Most people meet their long-term partners through their existing (real) social networks. Not many people have long-term relationships from meeting people in bars and clubs. So like Bella, your Edward or Jacob is most likely to be someone you meet through work, school or friends.

BEER GOGGLES

Everyone knows alcohol can make some look more physically attractive than they really are. Your judgement of a potential boyfriend will be skewed if your brain is affected by alcohol or drugs. You cannot judge a man accurately if you are drunk, any more than you can drive properly. If you have a great time with him when you are both under the influence, this doesn't mean you are necessarily suited for a relationship.

Drinking and dating can be as unwise as drinking and driving. Yet drinking alcohol with a prospective boyfriend is not only normal, it's positively encouraged.

Alcohol and drugs cause temporary brain dysfunction. You become a different person for a while. You may find him hilarious, when he isn't. Your powers of decision-making, control, and perception are altered. If he is under the influence too, you're not getting his true personality. He may seem funny, cheerful, carefree, confident. He may not be like this when sober.

In the same way that you can 'drink' a man good-looking, you can 'drink' him witty, intelligent, kind and fascinating. If you fall in love when you are drunk, you may fall in love with an illusion.

Pay attention to what your boyfriend is like when you and he are sober.

WHAT YOU CAN AND CAN'T LEARN ABOUT HIM FROM YOUR FIRST DATE

The first thing you learn about him is not how he generally behaves; it is how *he thinks he should behave* on a first date.

It's an important difference. Because he's following the rules of normal social behaviour, he's making an effort to be polite, considerate and to find common ground. This is why people, when they first meet someone, often go away with a good impression. But when they get to know the person better, they sometimes revise their opinion.

Pay attention to the negatives

If he doesn't follow the normal rules of respectful behaviour when meeting you for the first time, then run. If he is inconsiderate, ungenerous, moody, rude, snappy, or shows other negative behaviour to you, then this is good information about who he is. If he can't even suppress his negative character traits long enough for your first meeting, it's a very bad sign.

Often you can trace a relationship problem right back to the first meeting. To take something very obvious, the boyfriend who gets very drunk on a first date is likely to be someone who drinks too much. It's surprising how many girls ignore clues like this. But there are more subtle signs, too. For example, one girl complained her boyfriend was thoughtless and selfish. When she looked back to their first meeting, she realised he'd turned up late for the date without any apology, they'd ended up eating Chinese food even though she said she wasn't fond of it, and he left her to walk home alone through the dark streets.

On a first meeting, the positive aspects of his behaviour may not be permanent parts of his character. The negative aspects of his behaviour probably are.

Listen with an open mind

Of course you need to listen to what he says. Talking is one of the best ways to get to know a man. A man will usually do his best to impress and say positive things about himself. But some of the things he says may not be true. This may be because of lack of self-awareness, wishful thinking, or deliberate lies.

So when he tells you positive things about himself, keep an open mind. These positive things may be true, or they may not. If he says, 'I'm the best salesman in my team' or 'I'm a caring person' wait and see if the reality checks out with this. This may sound harsh, showing a lack of trust. But a man has to earn your trust. It's not something you can give just on the basis of words.

✳ CAN YOU TELL IF SOMEONE IS LYING?

There is no sure-fire way to tell if someone is lying or not.

People often believe that not looking you straight in the eye is a sign of lying. In fact, some liars make a point of looking you straight in the eye because of this myth. Paul Ekman, a psychologist and expert on lying, has discovered the following clues to deceit:

Micro expressions: When he is lying about how he feels, a fleeting expression of the emotion he is trying to conceal touches his face for a split second. For example, he insists he is totally over his ex, but for a second the corners of his mouth turn downwards.

Contradicting himself: Liars need a good memory. Although honest people sometimes contradict themselves, a liar is likely to do this more often.

Not using his hands: When telling the truth, people are likely to use their hands to make gestures. When lying, the use of gestures reduces or stops altogether.

Distancing language: When he talks about something, he doesn't talk about it directly, but in a way that puts him at a distance from the subject. For example, instead of saying a direct phrase like 'I didn't try to kiss your best friend', he might be less direct with 'I didn't do anything like that'.

Fake facial expressions: When someone is feeling a genuine emotion, the facial expression that goes with it does not last very long. For example, the emotion of surprise lasts less than a second. If you ask your boyfriend if he's cheated on you, and his look of surprise lasts more than a second, then it's probably faked. He's not really surprised you're asking him this question. You need to wonder why.

The above signs are not foolproof. They are just clues that may show someone is lying. And there are skilled liars that even highly trained experts can't detect.

The only reliable way to find out if someone is telling you the truth is to see if the facts prove them right.

If he says something negative about himself...

Sit up, and take notice! It is highly likely to be true.

It takes a lot for a man to tell you something negative about himself. They don't do this lightly, especially with a girl they are trying to impress. If he's saying something bad about himself, it probably has a solid foundation. He is trying to get across an important fact about who he is.

For example: if you meet a guy and he tells you he's not big on commitment, got a bad temper, he drinks too much, he's selfish, is a heartbreaker – believe it.

Too often girls ignore these clear messages. At the end of an unhappy relationship, a girl will dump a guy tearfully, saying, you're just too selfish/bad-tempered/commitment-phobic. The man will say, in a bewildered voice, but I *told* you I was selfish/bad-tempered/not big on commitment.

There is sometimes a strange perverseness in girls that they will pay a huge amount of attention to all the positive things a man is saying (which may or may not be true) and completely ignore all the negatives (which are highly likely to be true).

Why is this?

It may be because they are assuming a man is like a woman. Women are generally quite self-critical. Women often 'put themselves down' in conversation. For example, you might say to a female friend, 'I think I look terrible in this dress, it makes me look fat.' She's likely to reply, 'Oh no, it doesn't, you look great, the colour really suits you.' She comforts you and it's a way of bonding. We criticise ourselves and build each other up. It's a common way for females to communicate. You know for a fact when your female friend says something negative about herself, she is probably being self-critical and is expecting your reassurance.

Our mistake is to assume men are the same. But men are not brought up to put themselves down. It is the opposite: men are raised to 'puff themselves up', show off how great they are and to conceal any weakness. When he says something negative about himself, he's not being excessively self-critical. He's saying it because it's true. He's trying to be clear about what you can expect from him.

FINDING OUT MORE IN THE FOLLOWING WEEKS

After a successful first date, your task of paying close attention does not end. More information about your new love interest will be coming your way, so make sure you make use of it.

What do your family and friends say about him?

You may be thinking: but I like to make up my own mind about a person! Well, that's only natural. But you may be flattering yourself about your powers of perception.

Research has demonstrated that the more people put their minds to a question, the more accurate the answer. This is called the 'wisdom of crowds'. This is why on the TV show *Who Wants to be a Millionaire?* the lifeline 'Ask the Audience' is almost always more reliable than 'Phone a Friend'. One person's judgment is more likely to be wrong than the combined judgment of a whole crowd of people.

Within the first few weeks of dating a guy, you are likely to introduce him to your best friend, sister or other family members, or meet up in a circle of friends. It's a good idea to ask your friends and family if they have any doubts or worries about him. Ask for their views of his bad points, as well as what they like about him. Try not to just dismiss other people's views; think about them carefully.

If several people are giving you a negative message about your man, it has a good chance of being true. Listening to other people is the smart thing to do. Then you can make up your mind.

✱ HOW LONG SHOULD YOU WAIT BEFORE ✱ YOU KNOW IF HE IS 'THE ONE'?

Professor Ted Huston, a researcher at the University of Texas, has found that couples are unlikely to stay together if they have a short, whirlwind courtship of less than a year and rush into marriage while on a romantic 'high'. He found that these couples, although they experienced intense passion, had an idealised view of each other and therefore became slowly disillusioned over the course of their marriage. According to Professor Huston, long-lasting relationships are based not so much on hot passion, but on a cooler, but more enduring warmth and a realistic understanding of each other. He believes that short courtships can sometimes lead to a lasting marriage if couples have a solid foundation for a relationship and can accurately judge when they are right for each other.

However, the couples in his studies most likely to stay together had been dating for around two years, four months.

Professor Huston believes that a courtship can be too long, though. He found that couples who waited more than four years before committing were also at high risk of splitting up. He thinks that there was a good reason why these couples delayed marriage: they were not convinced about the relationship, and they turned out to be right.

Listen to your intuition

Professor Richard Wiseman, a psychologist, has investigated the difference between women who were lucky in love and those who were unlucky.

He describes his discoveries in his book *The Luck Factor*. He found the big difference between them was that the girls who were lucky in love listened to their intuition. If their inner voice said something wasn't right about a man, they moved on. Those who were unlucky in love ignored their inner voice and carried on seeing a man who wasn't right for them. Professor Wiseman believes your inner voice or your gut feelings can often be more perceptive than your conscious mind. If you are uncomfortable, or something doesn't feel right about a man, pay attention to this, even if you can't pinpoint why you are feeling this way.

Intuition is important. You can enhance it by reading the next chapter.

CHAPTER 15

HOW TO LEARN MORE ABOUT YOUR BOYFRIEND

Girls who are lucky in love are good at realising early when a man is definitely NOT their Edward or Jacob. They have good intuition when it comes to spotting the warning signs that he's a man unlikely to make any girl happy.

Firstly, there are signals that should scream out 'Stay Away' to you with loud sirens and red flashing lights. Answering yes to any of the following means you are taking a huge risk with your happiness and even your physical well-being by being with him:

- Does he show signs of excessive drinking, gambling or drug addiction?
- Does he/has he engaged in criminal behaviour?
- Does he have a history of violence?
- Does he have anger problems?
- Has he hit/assaulted any of his exes?
- Has he been cruel to animals or children?
- Has he fathered children and abandoned them without contributing to their upbringing?
- Does he have any other pattern of behaviour that is antisocial or shows callousness or indifference to others' suffering?
- Is he refusing professional help for serious mental health problems?

The list above may seem obvious to you but a huge number of women do not pay enough attention to certain worrying facts about their man. Why? One reason is that girls listen to the story behind the unpleasant facts. They are often heartbreaking stories that tug at the heartstrings. You may feel flattered that he has shared his innermost feelings with you.

People who do unacceptable things usually have a reason for doing them. If you listen to his explanation, you will feel empathy for him. There is an old saying: 'To understand, is to forgive.' It is true. In *Twilight*, when Edward explains his uncontrollable cravings for Bella's blood and his battle against them, she is full of sympathy. Even though he's telling her he wants to kill her, her overwhelming instinct is to feel sorry for him.

If your man shows signs of any of the above problems, it's safest not to stick around long enough to hear his explanation. You don't want to understand him or look behind the facts. You need to judge his unacceptable behaviour on face value, and get out. The chances of such a man making you happy are very small indeed.

You may be asking, 'Isn't that being judgmental?' Yes it is! You need to be when choosing a boyfriend. It is probably one of the most important decisions of your life when it comes to your future happiness, well-being and even safety. It is not a time to be non-judgmental.

HOW DOES HE SEE WOMEN?

A man can be attractive in all sorts of ways – but if he doesn't like women very much, you are onto a loser. A man cannot love what he doesn't even like. Signs of a negative attitude to women are contemptuous remarks, denigration or using offensive language about women such as 'slag' or 'bitch'. It's a good idea to pay attention to what he says about other girls. For example, is he always talking about women's appearances and seeing them as playthings or objects?

IS HE ONLY AFTER ONE THING?

Your real-life Edward or Jacob is someone who is capable of and interested in being a 'one woman man'.

As you know, some men are not interested in monogamous relationships. These men are known as womanisers or 'players'. All they want is no-strings sex, and when they are bored with one girl they will move on. They may lose interest after one night, or they may want to see you for a few weeks. If they stay in a relationship, they are likely to be unfaithful. Falling in love with a womaniser is a road to heartbreak. It's best to spot them before you get emotionally involved.

Signs he could be a 'player':

- He has a reputation for being (or past behaviour shows that he is) a womaniser.
- He pays you excessive compliments on your appearance and clothes.
- He appears highly fascinated by you and is very charming.
- He creates emotionally charged conversations, encouraging you to open up and reveal your feelings. He is prematurely creating intimacy – he wants you to see him as a sexual partner as soon as possible.
- He says that he's falling in love with you after only one or two dates. Men do fall in love faster than women – but this is too fast.
- He first approached you (and this includes on social networking sites) without any non-verbal or verbal signs of interest from you. This is the dating equivalent

of 'spamming'; if he asks lots of girls out, sooner or later one will say yes.

- He acts coldly towards you if you pull away when he gets too friendly.
- He doesn't want to go out with you but wants to get you round to his house.

One way of finding out whether a man is only after one thing is to not get physical with him for a long time. The ones who are only looking for a short-term fling will probably lose interest.

Bella knew Edward was not a 'player' from his reputation – Jessica told her Edward had never looked at any of the girls in the school. And nor was Jacob interested in anyone else, until he imprinted on Renesmee. This is another reason why we love the *Twilight* heroes so much – they are faithful men. Not all men are so inclined!

THE TRUTH BEHIND HIS WORDS

The truth about a person is revealed through their actions far more than through their words. Talk is cheap. A man's behaviour says a lot about his true character, so pay far more attention to what he does than what he says.

For example, suppose you like to live healthily and eat well. He hears you mentioning this and responds by saying physical fitness is important to him. But if he never does any exercise and is always in the pub, you can tell where his priorities really lie.

Body language, tone of voice and facial expression often tell more truth than his words. If he is frowning and his body is tense, then he is very likely to be feeling angry; even if he assures you he is not, his non-verbal signals are probably more reliable than his words.

Try to notice patterns in his behaviour that are repeated in different ways in different situations. When you have spotted these you will know they are part of who he is and that he's likely to behave that way in the future.

WHAT ARE THE IMPORTANT THINGS ABOUT A MAN?

The rest of this chapter is a list of important aspects of a man to pay attention to, if you are looking for a serious boyfriend. It doesn't include absolutely everything that might be relevant to you. You may want to add more, based on your insights into yourself and what you need. The aim of this list is just to help you understand your boyfriend better over time; it is not a 'shopping list' of features he must have.

And I am not suggesting you analyse him, or rate him on questionnaires, or quiz him on these questions like an interviewer. Just get to know him naturally through normal conversation while paying attention to who he is.

His basic personality traits

His levels of negative emotion: how prone is he to bad moods? How often and how much does he get stressed out, upset, irritated? How often and how able is he to be calm and relaxed?

His ability to get on with others: how well does he harmonise and cooperate with other people?

Introversion: is he an extravert/introvert or somewhere in between?

His intellect: is he very down to earth, or does he enjoy imagination and abstract ideas?

His conscientiousness: is he neat, organised, with a strong sense of duty – or untidy, laid-back and spontaneous?

Integrity: how often does he do what he says he's going to do? How much can he be relied upon? What is his sense of right and wrong? Is he flexible in terms of his morals to the point where it could be a problem for you, or is he very proper and upright?

His self-esteem: does he put himself down, is he generally confident or is he a bit on the arrogant side?

His flexibility: how does he cope when plans are changed or people oppose his wishes?

His life satisfaction: is he happy enough with his lot, or has he got a chip on his shoulder and feels the world owes him more?

The emotions which drive him most

To understand him better it can help to notice the emotions that drive him most.

His positive feelings:

1) What gives him the greatest happiness? They may be very different to the things in life that make you happy.

2) What is he proud of? Notice what he takes great pride in, and how much this drives him.

3) What gives him the most amusement and physical pleasure? To understand your boyfriend it helps to have an insight into the enjoyment he takes from life.

4) What gives him contentment? What is his idea of relaxation and contented life?

5) What gives him the most satisfaction? The activities or interests that satisfy him are likely to be an important part of what makes him tick.

6) What does he find exciting and how much excitement does he like? He may seek excitement, or may prefer a quiet life. The kinds of things he finds exciting will tell you something about him.

His negative emotions:

Part of who he is includes negative emotions, too. Taking notice of these will help you understand him better.

1) Contempt: who does he look down on and why? Understanding who and what he feels contempt towards will tell you about his attitudes to people. Beware if he seems contemptuous towards girls!
2) Anger: what makes him angry? The amount and type of things that move him to anger are vital to consider if you are thinking of becoming his girlfriend.
3) Sadness: what makes him sad? Most people are sad when they lose someone or something. How often and what type of sadness your boyfriend experiences may be an important part of his character.
4) Fear: what is he afraid of? Men typically like to see themselves as physically brave, but men have fears just as much as women. For example, he may be scared of failure, humiliation, losing face, or being seen as weak.
5) Guilt: what does he feel guilty about? He might feel excessive guilt, or not enough.
6) Shame/embarrassment: what makes him ashamed or embarrassed? A man is likely to hide these feelings from you, at least in the early days. But his feelings of shame/embarrassment give you a clue as to how he sees himself and the areas he is sensitive about.

Other considerations

Education: what are his level of education and his ambitions? How important is education to him?
Work: you can't necessarily judge a man's character on the basis of his job. You can't assume a nurse is caring or a doctor is clever. There have been some cruel nurses and slow-witted doctors. But as your man will probably spend most of his life at work, it is a big part of

him. What is his attitude to work? And what does his choice of work say about him?

Politics: how interested is he in politics? Is he right-wing, left-wing, somewhere in between, Green or Monster Raving Loony Party?

Spirituality: how much of a part does religion play in his life? What religion does he follow? What does he believe in?

His leisure time: what newspapers, websites, films, books, music does he like? What hobbies, interests, sports does he enjoy?

Social class: what kind of background does he come from and how much is this part of who he is?

His social life: who he chooses to spend his spare time with can give you an insight into his personality. The amount and quality of the friendships tells you about his sociability. And the type of friends he has will mirror something about him. For example, if his friends are kind and trustworthy, there's a good chance your boyfriend is similar.

His passions: out of everything that might drive your man, there may be some aspects that really stand out. What are the things he engages in or talks about above all others?

His health/lifestyle: humans are physical beings and much of our time is taken up with maintaining our bodies. His attitudes towards and behaviour around smoking, exercise, diet, drinking and drugs are the important lifestyle factors to consider.

His activity/energy levels: how active does he like to be?

His attitude to money: what is his income now and his earning potential? Is he careful or does he let money slip through his fingers? How important is money to him? What are his financial ambitions?

His goals in life

To understand him as a person it helps to know where he is heading (or where he hopes to be heading). His goals can give you a clue about his values and what drives him as a person. Who he admires, his role models or men he holds in high esteem may tell you something about his values and who he aspires to be. If he doesn't have any goals in life, other than to have a great time, then this tells you a lot about him, too.

Other things that are important:

His sense of humour: humour is an important social bond. If you can laugh together, you will not only enjoy each other's company but it will also help you get through the bad times. Despite all the difficulties, Bella could share moments of humour with both Edward and Jacob. This strengthened their relationships and helped them face problems together.

How he copes in adversity: if your man becomes a long-term boyfriend you will probably have to face some tough things together as well as the good times. An important side to someone's character is how they cope.

If you have a chance to see him deal with something difficult, then this is a great opportunity to get to know him better. If everything is going well for him, you won't see this. But I wouldn't recommend secretly ordering his car to be towed away and crushed just to see how he copes with stress.

Some men are all sweetness and light when everything is going their way, but then turn into ogres, blame everyone else and create hell for others if something goes wrong.

How does he cope with pressure or obstacles? How does he cope with failure, setbacks or disappointments?

One of the reasons we recognise Edward and Jacob as heroes is that, on the whole, they face their problems with determination and courage, and keep Bella's best interests at heart.

How much he's willing to give... and take: life as a human being is a balancing act between giving to others and taking from them. Bella is a 'giver'. She is willing to give up everything for those she loves. Is your man a 'giver' or a 'taker' – or a reasonable balance of both?

His complaints about his ex: it's a good idea to listen to these very carefully. His complaints about his ex might tell you something about him. Some girls are all too happy to hear negative things about the ex-girlfriend – after all, you want him to love you best. You may be tempted to take his complaints at face value, and believe that his ex must be selfish, a killjoy, boring, greedy for his money, self-obsessed or whatever he is saying about her.

But his complaints may say more about him than her. You only have his side of the story. For example, it might be true that his ex was greedy for his cash… or it might be that he's mean with money.

Complaining about his ex is probably his way of signalling what he wants from you. Instead of hearing complaints, listen for the message. He's hoping you'll be better than her in these ways. He's giving you a warning about the kinds of things he doesn't like in a girl.

How he interacts with other people: he will behave differently with a crowd of people than when he's only with you. You are likely to see a different side of him.

Look at how he behaves with your friends, his friends, your family. How he treats them is just as important as how he treats you. If he's rude, dismissive, contemptuous, unpleasant or aggressive, then this is part of who he is as a person. The 'real him' is not just the person he is when he's alone with you. The side he shows to others is just as much a part of who he is.

How he behaves towards the helpless: seeing how he interacts with animals or small children can tell you something about the extent of his compassion and kindness… or lack of it.

HOW MUCH DO YOU NEED TO KNOW ABOUT A MAN?

The above list is not the be-all and end-all for getting to know a man deep down. There is no foolproof way of completely understanding another person – the above are just some things you might want to consider. You can't judge another person by a 'cookbook' of techniques. As long as you are making a genuine attempt to pay attention to who he really is, that is the main thing that matters.

It will take a long time to truly understand him. You don't have to know absolutely everything about him, and there's no need to be too analytical. Your feelings will show you whether you want to see more of him or not, not your logic. But if your feelings are based on a reasonably good understanding of who he is, you will save yourself some heartbreak and disappointment. Some clear signals about him and his personality will become apparent in the first few weeks – if you are paying attention. If you then like what you can see you can learn more and more in the months to come.

SECRET FIVE: SUMMARY

How to get a deep insight into your boyfriend:

- Recognise the warning signs of a man who won't make you happy.
- Understand the common pitfalls in judging men.
- Pay attention to all the information you have.
- Listen to what he's telling (and not telling) you.
- Understand his personality and emotions.

If you are self-aware and have a good idea about who he is then you have the foundations. You are a ready to move to the next step – are you really suited to each other?

How to Know if Your Relationship Really Works

(Learning from Edward and Bella)

CHAPTER 16

ARE YOU SUITED TO EACH OTHER?

THE EARLY DAYS

From their very first meeting, Edward looked at Bella with eyes full of hate. He wanted to kill her. In their relationship he was controlling and locked her up 'for her own safety', they argued constantly, he broke her heart and nearly destroyed her, she committed acts of self-harm just to hear a hallucination of his voice, he tried to commit suicide... true love doesn't look anything like this in real life. Love is wonderful in the beginning.

If you are well suited, the early days in a relationship should be fun – not hard work at all. You are both showing your best side to each other. You are both making special efforts to please. You are discovering common ground and delighting in your similarity and compatibility. You are both doing your best to bewitch each other. You are both avoiding conflict by being obliging.

This is your 'honeymoon period'. Couples who go on to have lasting, positive relationships are almost always very happy with each other in the beginning. The start of your relationship is the best it's ever going to be in terms of those exciting, carefree days of new romance.

If it's hard work or painful from the beginning then this is a bad sign. It's unlikely to improve. When troubled couples seeking help trace their unhappiness right back to the beginning, and can't remember the good times, this usually spells the end. It's hard to fix something that was never right in the first place.

The honeymoon period is the reality of the natural progression of romantic relationships. Unfortunately, it's also the exact opposite of what you might have been led to believe in romantic films and books. In fiction, the hero and heroine typically clash terribly at first, or can't abide each other, or push each other away. Then by the end of the story this is resolved and they become blissfully happy.

But in your own real-life love story, in the beginning of your relationship, you need to ask yourself: are you really enjoying your time together?

WHAT KIND OF MAN WILL MAKE YOU HAPPY?

In the last chapter I talked about understanding your boyfriend as a person. But what should you be looking for in a partner?

It goes without saying you need a man you find physically attractive, and a man you have some chemistry with. If this is missing, then you've found a male friend, not a boyfriend. As much as you like someone, if the physical attraction isn't there for you, he is not likely to make you happy.

But physical attraction is only part of a relationship. There are other important things to consider, and certain traits in particular are associated with long-term, successful, loving relationships.

Here are five traits to look out for:

1) Happiness

Your true love is likely to be, basically, a happy man. Research has shown the men who are happy in long-term relationships were likely to be happy when they were single. It's not too difficult to spot signs of happiness! He will be enthusiastic, say positive things about his life and comment on how much he enjoys things. He will smile and laugh frequently. Happiness is infectious. He will make you feel upbeat, too. Happy people generally have pretty good self-esteem. He's unlikely to have serious problems with his self-image.

He won't be happy all the time, of course. Everyone has times they feel fed up or stressed. But if he is an essentially happy person he won't feel negative emotions too often. Research shows that people are happier with partners who are not prone to feeling negative emotions like anger, anxiety and sadness.

2) Flexibility
A boyfriend who is high in flexibility is likely to make you happy. He will be able to cope with people disagreeing with him, or things not turning out as expected. When you and he clash, he will also make some attempt to see your point of view. He won't sulk for days or fly into a terrible temper if he doesn't get his way.

3) Ability to be forgiving
If he can forgive your faults and move on, you will be happier with him. In a long-term, loving relationship the ability to forgive and forget is essential. If he's judgmental and unforgiving it'll be a struggle being his girlfriend.

4) Agreeableness
Studies show partners high in agreeableness are more likely to make their loved one happy. So the ability to make you feel at ease, to be interested in you, to be in touch with your emotions are traits that will make you happy. The tendency to be aloof, hostile, aggressive or critical is associated with unhappy relationships. A good boyfriend is likely to be good at relationships generally. On the whole, he'll be good at harmonising with people.

5) Positive view of women
A loving partner will have a positive view of women. They will like girls and get on with them well.

Notice anything about these five characteristics? The kind of guy who will make you happy is: contented, flexible, forgiving, friendly and gets on well with girls. In other words, he is the *exact opposite* of the classic romantic hero.

The kind of guy who will make you miserable is: deeply unhappy, inflexible, dislikes himself, is judgmental, aloof, despises girls, doesn't get on well with people and is generally hostile or critical of others. In other words, the typical dark hero in romantic fiction.

The dark hero type is not likely to make you happy. But why are some girls attracted to the unhappy, inflexible, aloof guy? One reason is that this kind of behaviour is typical of dominance.

Next time you are in a situation where there is a hierarchy of power, look at the behaviour of the person at the top, and compare this with the people lower down in the pecking order. It's likely the big boss will smile less, be more aloof, respond less to people's emotions, be more openly critical and show more hostile expressions such as frowning, looking down their nose or scowling. Think of Alan Sugar in *The Apprentice*, or Simon Cowell on *The X Factor*.

Women are attracted to these kind of men. Women are typically attracted to power. It's probably in your genes – if your ancestors pair-bonded with powerful men in their social groups, their babies were more likely to survive.

But you need to make a distinction between the man who is showing dominant behaviour because he has genuinely high status, and the guy who is just a bit of a bully or is unhappy with poor social skills.

 Izzy, whose story is in Chapter 10, had been attracted to her boyfriend Keiran because she thought he was strong and powerful, but in reality he was just a troubled

and insecure man. He became controlling, then violent, almost strangling her. After this traumatic experience, Izzy worked on changing the way she approached relationships.

'I knew I was attracted to men who were moody, complicated and domineering. Keiran had a dark, brooding look and I was drawn to him. Another boyfriend had been the scowling type, too. I thought they were fascinating. It felt as if they were powerful, mysterious men. But there was no mystery. I can see now that these brooding, scowling men were just ordinary people who weren't very good at getting on with others.'

Their domineering behaviour didn't make her happy. She set out to be more thoughtful about who she was attracted to. When she next felt drawn to a man, she talked it over with her best friend Philippa. If she realised she was being attracted to a difficult man who needed help, she walked away. It wasn't easy.

Then a new colleague, David, came to work at her firm. 'To be honest, I didn't really pay any attention to him at first, other than to note he was really attractive. He was a cheerful guy who people liked, always quick with a funny comment. I didn't talk to him much, though, until we worked on a project together, selling display space for a brand new exhibition.'

She discovered he was a straightforward, hard-working man who enjoyed life. There was no dramatic, mysterious or compelling story about his background. 'I found myself enjoying his company. I felt comfortable with him. David was happy and relaxed, and didn't even get stressed when I screwed up my half of the project. I was panicking and thought he'd be furious, but he just made a joke of it – he laughed and said I reminded him *of the "startled kitty" on YouTube – and helped sort things out.'*

Looking from the outside, it was clear to others that they had a lot in common – they were both outgoing people who liked parties and socialising. Neither was naturally academic but both worked hard and were becoming successful in their careers. But it took a while before Izzy broke out of her old rut of looking for brooding, mysterious men.

'We've started dating. I find myself getting nervous when David asks what I'm up to, because I see it as being interrogated. But he's just asking out of interest. Sometimes he doesn't understand why I'm so jumpy and I haven't explained yet. He calls me his crazy cat. He's pretty happy with me, I think. He smiles a lot and it's a rare moment when he isn't cheerful. That's pretty nice, knowing someone is always ready to laugh with you.'

WHO IS YOUR SOULMATE?

True love is not just about the two tasks of finding a man who is free of characteristics that would make him a bad partner, while looking for signs that he's capable of being a good partner. There is more to it than this. True love is about finding someone who is very compatible with you.

On the whole, research on relationships shows that couples who are similar to each other are happier. So your real-life Edward or Jacob will be like you in terms of background, goals, interests and values. Hollywood may lead you to think love can bind chalk and cheese together, but the truth is it can't. Couples who match more closely with each other are happier than mismatched couples. And couples who share a lot in common are more likely to stay together.

People who find true love often call their partner their 'soulmate' or their 'other half'. In an ancient myth, human beings were cut in two by the gods to punish them. So their souls and bodies were divided into two. For the rest of eternity, they wandered the earth, looking for the other half to their soul. Sex was the way they temporarily reunited the two halves of their selves. This is only a myth, but it illustrates a basic truth. Your true love will be a twin soul – he will be similar to you.

BUT DON'T OPPOSITES ATTRACT?

Yes, they do – for a while. But opposites do not seem to gel together in the long term. Research shows that couples very different from each other are less likely to stay together.

Interestingly, research has also revealed that people attracted to an 'opposite' have, on average, lower self-esteem to those attracted to someone similar. Why is this? It could be that, as they don't respect themselves, people with low self-esteem value people who have qualities opposite to themselves. It may be they look for qualities in a partner that make up for their perceived deficiencies. For example, if you've never been confident about your academic ability, you may be attracted to someone who seems intelligent.

In the *Twilight* series, Bella was particularly clumsy and physically awkward. She was very attracted to the poised, elegant Edward. She was socially unskilled and aloof, so she was attracted to the easy-going warmth and friendliness of Jacob.

The problem with opposites attracting is that in the long term, similarities work better than differences. Life together across the years means doing things in common, looking at things in the same way, and sharing the same abilities and desires.

If you are attracted to a man because he is the opposite of you, it's less likely that he is your soulmate.

ARE YOU COMPATIBLE?

The early days are the chance to get to know each other better and find out how compatible you are as a couple. Your real-life Edward or Jacob is likely to be similar to you in the areas which may be important to you, such as the following:

- Education
- Spirituality
- Intellectual style
- Introversion/extroversion
- Conscientiousness
- Attitude to work
- Attitude to money
- Sense of humour
- View on politics
- Leisure interests
- Social class
- Life goals
- Passions
- Health/lifestyle factors
- Morals/values
- Activity/energy levels
- The things in life that give you positive emotions
- The things in life that give you negative emotions.

As you get to know each other, you'll discover whether you are both on the same page in the areas that matter.

LISTEN TO YOUR INTUITION

Sometimes, on paper, everything seems fine. You find him physically attractive. He doesn't show any of the warning signs that you need to avoid. You are similar in all of the important areas of personality, goals, priorities, interests, background, outlook, values and so on. He seems like a man capable of making you happy. But your intuition tells you something isn't quite right...

The way a man makes you feel can hold important information. If they are negative emotions, ignore them at your peril. If you feel a strong negative emotion when you are with a man, listen to your intuition. When Bella was with Edward, she felt fear time and time again. She ignored this. This doesn't matter in a story, but it's not a good idea in real life.

THE DIFFERENCES BETWEEN YOU

Of course there will be some differences between you. He is a man and you are a woman for a start! All humans are unique and you are bound to be different in plenty of respects. So the question is: how can you tell which differences make you incompatible and which don't?

The relationship expert Dr John Gottman says that in any couple there are two basic types of difference:

1) The first type he calls the 'situational difference'. This is the type of difference that is probably temporary, and can be resolved by changes in circumstances.
2) The second he calls the 'perpetual difference'. This is a difference between you that is a fundamental difference in personality or lifestyle. It will probably never change.

For example, imagine you are going out with a man who is struggling for money at the moment. He is doing an apprenticeship and has to look after every penny. You've been promoted at work, and now have more money to spend. You are keen to book a holiday. He is more cautious. He'd love to go on holiday too, but doesn't really have the money and doesn't want you to pay for it all because he doesn't want to feel like a kept man. You get impatient – you've worked hard and are really looking forward to a break. You argue.

This is a situational difference. Once he's qualified, your differences will disappear. You are likely to harmonise about money. You both want to do similar things with your money – a holiday is what you would both choose. When he's earning a good salary you're not likely to be so very different.

But take this scenario:

Nicky and Jack have been seeing each other for four weeks, have great chemistry and are enjoying getting to know each other. They have a shared passion for movies and are physically compatible. However, they are just discovering they have differences on the topic of money...

Nicky has a relaxed attitude. Spend now, worry later is her philosophy. She racks up her credit card bill to the maximum and thinks a credit limit unused is a credit limit wasted. Jack would rather jump in a lake than leave a credit card bill unpaid. He's awake all night fretting if he feels he's paid too much for a second-hand jacket bought on eBay. He'd take an old loaf of bread, cut the mould off and make a sandwich for lunch, while Nicky would be popping into the local bistro and raising a glass of Prosecco to toast her benefactors at Visa and MasterCard. Jack wants to save up enough money to put it into a really high-interest savings account. Nicky wants to take out another credit card so she can book a holiday in the Maldives. Jack is privately beginning to think Nicky is completely irresponsible about money, Nicky is beginning to suspect Jack is a miser...

If they carry on seeing each other, how long will they be arguing about money for? Probably until they split up.

This is a 'perpetual difference'. No matter how much money they have, there is a fundamental difference between them about the way it should be spent. It's unlikely Jack and Nicky have found true love. The perpetual difference between them is just so huge that they will probably never find happiness with each other. Studies show that couples who have big differences about money are less happy together.

If you are arguing about a major incompatibility like this, he may not be your true love.

But don't all couples have arguments, I hear you ask. Yes, they do. And the arguments you have can tell you a lot about your relationship. There are secrets lying hidden in your very first argument that can give you a clue whether you've found your Edward or Jacob.

CHAPTER 17

WHAT YOUR ARGUMENTS SAY ABOUT YOUR RELATIONSHIP: BELLA'S FIGHTS WITH EDWARD

Bella and Edward disagreed with each other throughout the *Twilight* saga. One of their biggest fights was near the beginning of *Eclipse*. Bella had gone to La Push to visit Jacob against Edward's wishes and when he found out, he was furious. He felt she'd risked her life and put him in danger of breaking the treaty between the vampires and the werewolves. Bella was angry with Edward for expecting her to stay away from Jacob. They confronted each other and had a huge, emotional argument.

Conflict is a vital part of good fiction, and also a part of any good relationship. But the kind of arguments you have can give you clues as to whether you are destined to stay together... or to part.

A SECRET EVERY GIRL SHOULD KNOW...

Your first disagreement is important, so it's a good idea to pay attention to it. It marks the transition between the honeymoon period and a proper boyfriend/girlfriend relationship. Or it might mark the beginning of the end of your time together as a couple.

The first argument doesn't have to be a negative thing. All couples have differences in opinion. Finding that your feelings for each other are strong enough to weather the storm of a conflict shows you're beginning to really gel together. The ability to resolve those differences, kiss and make up is the sign of a strong relationship. And it's a sign you are both maturing from the superficial attraction phase into a deeper, loving one.

So it can be a very good thing.

Alternatively, your first argument might be a signal that:

- He is dangerous.
- You have fundamental incompatibilities as a couple.
- One or both of you don't cope well with conflict.
- Your feelings for each other are not strong enough to withstand the stress of arguments.

How can you tell which? There's no foolproof way to predict the future, but the kind of thing you have conflicts about and the way you fight can give clues as to how well suited you are as a couple.

DANGER SIGNALS

It goes without saying that if your boyfriend uses physical force against you in your first argument, then he is not your Edward or Jacob. Even if you love him, you need to end the relationship immediately. There is no benefit of the doubt with violence. No matter how sorry he is, no matter how compelling a reason he has for explaining his behaviour, it has to end there. He has assaulted you. A real-life Edward or Jacob would not dream of hurting you. You may want to report him to the police and seek support. Ending a relationship with a man who is violent is risky and you may need help.

Even if your first argument doesn't end in violence, there may be other signs of danger. The following can be early warning signs of violence to come:

- He displays excessive anger, such as shouting, swearing or breaking things.
- He uses his physical strength; for example, controlling you physically with a push or pulling you along by the arm.
- He gets very angry about something minor.
- He feels humiliated or insulted in a way that is out of proportion to the situation.
- He blames you entirely for his unhappiness.
- He has a sudden, inexplicable change in his mood.
- He questions you excessively about where you've been.
- He overturns your decisions without negotiating with you first.
- He justifies controlling behaviour by saying it's to protect you, or because he loves you so much.
- He shows excessive jealousy or insecurity.

Edward showed some of these warning signs. Bella complained that he was 'pushy'. For example, when she went to drive home after fainting in biology, he grabbed her by the jacket and towed her along, ignoring her when she demanded he let go. He justified this as being for her own good. But the adults at school were happy for her to drive home. If he didn't like it, he could have used persuasion or argument, but the choice whether or not to drive home was entirely up to her, as a free agent.

As their romantic relationship developed, he showed increasingly controlling behaviour, ending in keeping her prisoner at his house.

All this was done with the reason of 'protecting' Bella.

In the real world, there is a big problem with having a boyfriend who feels he can violate your personal freedom in order to 'protect' you. The attempts to control often escalate into violence.

There is a chance that one day he will be the person you'll need most protection from.

ORDINARY BOYFRIEND/GIRLFRIEND ARGUMENTS

Most arguments between couples are not violent.

For the more usual type of conflict, it can be useful to look at whether your first argument arises out of a situational or a perpetual difference between you. In other words, is your argument about something temporary, which can be solved by changing the situation? Or would solving it require one of you to change your personality, tastes, personal expectations or lifestyle?

Sometimes it's not easy to know the difference. See if you can tell which is which in the following example. Remember Jazz the guitar player, the girl in Chapter 9 who fell in love with Alan?

> *'Our first argument was when Alan's parents were coming for Sunday lunch at his flat. We were going to cook for them together and it was the first time we'd hosted anything like that as a couple. I remember I was trying to finish writing a new song and was wishing I had time to be alone.'*
>
> *Jazz went shopping for food while Alan cleaned up his flat. 'When I was out I walked past an art shop. In the window they had a huge canvas showing a distorted view of an abandoned children's playground, weeds sprouting up under the slides and vines climbing up the swings. One of those pictures that really speak out loud, you know? I walked back to Alan's flat with lyrics forming in my head. I love it when that happens.*
>
> *'I let myself in and was telling Alan all about it. He wasn't listening; he was rummaging through the*

supermarket bags. I started telling him the lyrics and he interrupted me. "Did you get sprouts?" he kept asking. I couldn't remember if I'd got them or not, and didn't care either way. I kept on about my song and he kept on about sprouts and how his parents always loved their sprouts with a Sunday dinner.

'The lyrics for my song just vanished from my head. Gone. Replaced with thoughts of vegetables. Have you ever tried to write a song about sprouts? Exactly. We had this frantic argument, with him blaming me and me blaming him. When his parents arrived you could cut the tension with a plastic spoon.

'Looking back, it seems an insane thing to have a first argument about. Though, to be fair, I had forgotten the sprouts. And his parents were a bit disappointed.'

Was this argument because of a situational difference or a perpetual difference?

This was a perpetual difference. Jazz was happy when she felt she had a rich, creative inner life. To Jazz, creating a song was far more important than day-to-day practicalities. Alan had a mind that was far more down to earth. He liked to see concrete results from taxing his brain: to him, talking about a song that doesn't even exist was a bit of a waste of time. He wanted to sort out the real-life problem of entertaining his parents.

This was a permanent difference between them. Alan could not change his nature to become more imaginative and unorthodox. Jazz could not change hers to become more conventional and practical. They had this same row, in different forms, until the end of their relationship.

This list doesn't cover everything. Dr John Gottman estimates that 69 per cent of all couples' differences are perpetual. This means the chances are that most of the differences between you can't be solved.

But this doesn't mean you can't have a happy relationship. All couples have some perpetual differences. You can't solve the problem by eliminating your differences, but you can compromise and come to some agreement on how you handle them.

If your first argument shows there's a perpetual difference between you, the question becomes: can you come to some arrangement between you to handle it?

For example, Jazz and Alan could have recognised that they were different intellectually. They could have adjusted their expectations of each other. Jazz could have stopped expecting Alan to be excited when she was writing a new song, and Alan could have stopped expecting Jazz to be as practical as him. They could have worked on letting their partner be themselves.

TOO MUCH OF A GOOD THING...

Your boyfriend may have some great qualities. These merits attracted you to him in the first place. But the trouble is, every positive has its pitfall – if that good quality is taken too far.

For example, remember Suzi in Chapter 8? Her ex, Cam, was lively and fun and always cracking jokes. He had a quip for every situation and she liked that about him. But sometimes he took this quality too far. He joked in situations when he should have shown respect – such as her aunt's funeral.

One of the things Bella liked about Edward was the way he loved to take care of her. But he liked to take care of her too much, and it spilled over into control. His urge to protect became overprotection. This was his pitfall.

As for Jacob, she loved his easy, warm, spontaneous affection. But Jacob overdid this, and showed affection and tried to kiss her when she didn't want him to.

Here are some more examples:

Good Quality	Pitfall
Honesty	Being too bluntly honest and hurting your feelings.
Generosity	Being so generous that people exploit him.
Kindness	Being so kind people take advantage of him.
Cheerfulness	He's so determined to be cheerful he refuses to face some negative realities.
He's rich	He's so rich you've had kidnap threats and every day you have to fight off a different size-zero blonde trying to get her claws into him.

Remember that you have pitfalls, too – your first argument might be about one of your pitfalls, not his. For example, perhaps he loves your fun-loving nature, zest for parties and socialising. But now he needs to buckle down to study or work, yet you keep pressurising him to go out.

Do you know what your own good qualities and pitfalls might be? To find out, it may help to discuss this with a close friend. Every good point you have has a downside if you take it too far.

YOUR EXPECTATIONS OF EACH OTHER AS BOYFRIEND AND GIRLFRIEND

When you go into a relationship, you have ideas about how a boyfriend should behave. And he has ideas about how a girlfriend should behave.

It's as if you've signed a contract with each other, agreeing to certain terms and conditions. You have expectations about the kind of roles you will play for each other. But the problem is – at first you don't really know what you've signed up to. Sometimes your expectations will clash:

- How *he* thinks he should behave as a boyfriend is different to how *you* think he should behave as a boyfriend.
- How *you* think you should behave as a girlfriend is different to how *he* thinks you should behave as a girlfriend.

Bella and Edward had clashing expectations about each other's role as boyfriend and girlfriend. Edward saw his role as protecting Bella's life at all costs. At the beginning of their relationship, he believed this was his duty and restricting her freedom was a reasonable price to pay.

Bella believed she had the right to risk her life and well-being as she saw fit, and that her freedom and choice in life should be respected by Edward, even if it meant she was in danger.

Many of their arguments were about this clash. This was the boyfriend/girlfriend contract that Edward might have signed:

My contract
Clause 1: As her boyfriend, it's my responsibility to keep Bella safe at all costs. It's my right to override her freedom of choice if necessary.
Clause 2: Bella has a duty to herself and to me to avoid all activities which might risk her well-being.
Signed: Edward Cullen

This would be the contract Bella signed:

My contract
Clause 1: As a girlfriend, I support Edward but still exercise my complete right to act as I see fit, even if it risks my well-being.

2: It's Edward's responsibility to respect my freedom and accept the risk I might be hurt.
Signed: Bella Swan

These unwritten rules are not easy to spot. Often you don't know what they are – until they are broken.

The more serious the relationship, the more you will expect from each other. These expectations come into full force when you are married or living together. What a man expects from a wife or live-in partner is usually a whole lot more than from a casual girlfriend. He might start expecting you to do home baking or iron his underpants. You might expect him to unblock the drains or re-grout the bathroom.

You can often get a clue as to how he expects a girlfriend to behave by getting to know his parents. His expectations of a woman's role are likely to be shaped by his parents' example. If he was brought up in a family where his mum worked and his parents shared the household chores and decisions equally, he will probably expect to do the same. But if he grew up in a household where his mother did all the domestic chores and deferred to his father, he may well expect similar from you.

But you can't tell for sure. This is why it's important to take time to get to know your man and his family. You don't know what he expects from you. It may be something you don't want to sign up to!

DO YOU HAVE GOOD OR BAD ARGUMENTS?

The relationship expert Dr John Gottman believes it's not so much *what* you argue about that's important, but *how* you argue.

Gottman has found that if you start your conflict off badly – by being critical or contemptuous in the first few minutes of the disagreement – then there's a 96 per cent chance your argument won't end well. The argument won't move you on, it won't 'clear the air', and it won't result in a solution. It'll result in failure, anger and resentment.

This 'harsh start-up' as Gottman calls it, or critical and contemptuous comments near the beginning of an argument, are not a good sign. If in your first argument your man (or you) kicks off with contempt or nasty criticism, then you both may struggle to sustain a loving relationship, unless you work on your ability to handle conflict.

When you disagree with each other, there are four negative styles of interaction. If your arguments persist in showing all four of them, you have a 90 per cent chance of splitting up. Gottman calls them the 'Four Horsemen of the Apocalypse' because they predict that your relationship may be doomed.

The Four Horsemen of the Apocalypse:
1) Criticism
Criticising is when you make remarks about your partner that are a general attack, instead of just describing their specific behaviour. For example, if your boyfriend hasn't tidied up, instead of saying, 'I thought you were going to sort this room out today,' you say, 'You never do anything I ask.'

2) Contempt
Non-verbal signs of contempt are the eye roll, or a sneering expression on the face with the downwards twist to the mouth. Verbal signs are using insulting language to each other. For example, if your boyfriend hasn't tidied up and you say, 'You're a lazy slob.'

3) Defensiveness
This is when you are trying to complain to your boyfriend, but he's knocking back everything you throw at him. He won't accept

that there's anything wrong with the way he behaves. 'But I tidy up more than you,' would be an example.

4) Stonewalling

This is the silent treatment, or some other sign that shows he is not listening. You feel like you are talking to a wall. For example, when he says, 'Whatever. What's for dinner?'

Bella and Edward were quite good at arguing. They didn't show many signs of the Four Horsemen. The worst insult Edward threw at Bella was in *Twilight*, when he called her 'utterly absurd' after she'd asked him if he was trying to irritate her to death.

HOW HAPPY COUPLES ARGUE

There are 'good' ways of arguing. This may sound odd, but you should feel optimistic about the future if you have an argument that is conducted in the 'right' way.

According to Gottman, the happy couple use a 'softened start-up'. This is where you open the conversation gently. Arguments often finish the way they start. If you begin by talking respectfully, the conflict is more likely to end amicably.

When happy couples argue, they will do something to repair the rift between them, such as make a positive comment, inject a bit of humour, or smile. The other person will respond positively.

Edward and Bella often made these 'repair' attempts. The first time they went to their clearing in the woods, they were both cross with each other. But in the middle of this Edward smiled at Bella, trying to get the positive connection back.

Another sign that you handle conflicts well is that you are both willing to compromise and are accepting of each other's faults.

Bella and Edward's relationship worked out happily because of a willingness to compromise. In the end, Edward was willing to compromise on his desire to control Bella and his wish to keep her human. Bella and Jacob stayed close friends, because Jacob was willing to compromise about his attitude to vampires.

Think back to a recent argument with a boyfriend. What were the comments like in the first few minutes? Were they respectful of each other, even though you were both cross? Were there moments where you were signalling that you liked each other, 'repair' attempts that showed you wanted to work things out?

THE HAPPINESS COUNT

A finding from John Gottman's research is that a happy relationship will have far more positive interactions than negative ones. Couples who stay together have plenty of times together where they are showing each other affection, interest, empathy, compliments, appreciation and kindness. For happy couples, the ratio of these positive things is five to one. So for every negative exchange they have, there are five good ones.

And super-happy couples have even more good times than this, with twenty positive interactions for every negative one.

Bella and Edward did seem to show lots of positive behaviour towards each other, despite their difficulties. According to Gottman, a couple can weather the storm of conflict, as long as there are plenty of good times as well.

So if your boyfriend is being positive towards you at least five times for every negative, this is a good sign. If you are having few positive interactions, it could be you haven't got a solid enough foundation of happiness, and he is not your Edward or Jacob.

MAYBE THINGS WILL CHANGE...

Couples have arguments because they want something to change. A successful argument often results in a change of some kind, where one or both of you adjust your behaviour or expectations.

Many of Bella and Edward's conflicts were about her wish to become a vampire. She knew their relationship wouldn't work if she stayed human. So she was willing to transform herself so they could be happy together. She had the option of making this change.

And Edward had great powers of transformation himself. He changed from someone who thirsted for Bella's blood into a gentle, loving partner.

But how much change can you expect in reality?

CHAPTER 18

DO YOU LOVE HIM AS HE IS?

DO YOU LOVE THE MAN UNDERNEATH?

A man can have a fantastic persona in public. He can appear caring, sensitive, intelligent, respectful, considerate, confident and charming. And he genuinely is – when he's interacting with people at a surface level of intimacy. On casual acquaintance you may get a great impression.

When you get to know him better, you pass through to deeper levels of intimacy and get closer to the real him. As he begins to reveal his more personal feelings, his real thoughts and reactions, you will get a better idea about who he is inside.

The person he is underneath may well be just as loveable as his public face. You may discover some faults and vulnerabilities, but these just make him more human and you love him despite, or even because of, them.

But the person he is underneath may be at odds with his public face. The man who is charming with strangers may be dismissive with his colleagues, unreliable to his friends and cruel to his girlfriend. On a deeper level, he may not have any great qualities at all.

Some girls fall in love with the public man, and once they have 'imprinted' on this side of him, they have great difficulty in seeing the reality of who their boyfriend really is. They may ignore, minimise or excuse his bad behaviour.

When trying to work out if a man may be your Edward or

Jacob, its useful to ask yourself whether you love the man as he really is deep down in his soul... or just his charming exterior.

DO YOU WANT TO CHANGE HIM?

You may say to yourself, 'He'd be perfect if only he...' or, 'We'll be really happy together when...'

Be honest. Do you really love him as he is right now? Or do you love your vision of who you think he could or should be?

Some girls don't love the reality of their boyfriend but are attached to some idea of who he could be if he fulfilled his potential. You may know a girl who has a boyfriend with no redeeming features at all. But she sees something you can't see: it is her image of who he could become. She has a vision for his future and she's fallen in love with it.

Seeing potential for change is a common female trait. It may be due to our nurturing nature. We have an awareness of how, with care and attention, people can develop. Women are closely involved with human growth. In *Breaking Dawn*, Stephenie Meyer observes that women's bodies change far more than men's. Women go through cycles every month, and physically change during pregnancy. We carry babies and help them grow into toddlers, small children, teenagers and young adults, under our loving care. The natural female instinct is to foster change. We are given to believe, from the thousands of love stories we've been exposed to (mostly written by women), that men too can transform themselves through a loving relationship.

If you love him not so much for who he is now, but who you imagine him becoming, then you may be letting yourself in for years of disappointment and pain.

There are limits on change for adult men. Men of any age don't like to be treated like a project or house in need of refurbishment. Most men like to stay the way they are; being forced to behave in a way that's contrary to their own inclinations takes great effort.

People accept they have to behave against their own nature when they're being paid for it. So the untidy, sloppy man is prepared to keep his workplace tidy if it's part of his job. The aggressive, hot-tempered man is prepared to behave with polite respect to his boss. The rude, uncaring man is willing to play the role of the understanding, patient customer relations worker, while he's being paid to do it. But when people are off duty, they like to revert to their natural way of being. They don't appreciate being 'moulded' by anyone.

Basic acceptance of your partner's underlying personality is essential in a happy relationship. If he doesn't feel loved as he is, if his fundamental self feels attacked or criticised, you won't be contented as a couple.

WHAT CAN BE CHANGED?

People do change and grow over their lives to a limited extent. One study found that people tend to get better organised during their twenties, and tend to get more agreeable in their thirties. The same study found that women usually get more relaxed over their lifetimes, whereas men are likely to continue feeling the same stress levels. However, on the whole, most research shows personality traits are quite stable over time.

Experienced therapists can help some people change aspects of their personality, if the person desperately wants to change, and if they commit to around two years of therapy and are prepared to work very, very hard. But it's not guaranteed even then.

As a girlfriend, you can't transform your boyfriend's basic personality. For example, imagine he's the highly conscientious, organised type. It's beginning to get on your nerves that he puts his CDs in alphabetical order and has a schedule worked out for your weekends together, down to the exact timings put aside for getting friendly on the sofa. It's unrealistic for you to expect him to completely transform. He is never going to be that spontaneous, freewheeling person you might like him to be. You may compromise together, and make allowances for each other's natures, but he won't change deep down. If you have a perpetual difference between you like this, fundamental change is not to be expected. Instead, you can hope for compromise.

BUT SURELY HE'LL CHANGE AS HE GROWS UP?

It's true that young men are often immature, playing pranks on each other, giggling and lounging around at home. Your boyfriend might show up late for dates or forget to call you because he was playing on his Xbox. You may shake your head and look forward to the time when he becomes more adult.

He will develop as he gets older. If your boyfriend is very young, then his potential for change and growth is greater. A teenager is likely to be trying out different roles, behaviour, attitudes and identities to see which ones fit him best. Research shows that teenagers do make shifts in personality traits. An immature guy in his early twenties might be the same.

Although a young guy may grow, he may not change in the direction you want him to. You might reasonably hope that an immature boyfriend becomes a little more considerate and organised as he gets older. But it's unwise to expect any dramatic changes. If he's immature and selfish, he is highly likely to become mature and selfish. If he's immature and kind, he is highly likely to become mature and kind.

CHANGE ISN'T EASY

We live in a time where striving for personal happiness through personal change is encouraged. It has become fashionable to believe we can be transformed through personal effort. In the old days people were likely to look to God to help them change. They prayed for divine help to overcome their shortcomings, to be stronger, more patient, or to avoid sin. As a race we have made enormous leaps in our understanding of the world and we now feel we can sort our problems out ourselves.

In the past, an unfaithful husband would have turned to the Church to pray for forgiveness and the strength to change. Nowadays, wronged wives pack their straying husbands off to 'counselling' instead.

Today many people put their faith in communication skills and psychological techniques. However, the advances in psychology are nowhere near as rapid as the advances in technology. The computer in your mobile phone today would have needed a building to house it 40 years ago, yet in the same period of time the methods employed to change human behaviour have not advanced greatly. Whatever type of therapy you use, many treatments fail. Psychological programmes for behaviour change have only modest success. The success rate for changing personality is very modest indeed.

Of course, some change is possible. There are some very useful psychological techniques. And you can work hard on changing yourself, if you want to do it. You can strive to overcome your fears, bad habits and negativity, and improve your confidence. This is within your power.

But it's not within your power to change another adult human being – no matter what the love stories say.

EDWARD'S TRANSFORMATIONS

The *Twilight* saga is about the conflicts between Bella, Edward and Jacob and how they are resolved. But the story gives an exaggerated view of the changes possible – it is after all a romance, in the sense of containing 'improbable and extravagant lies'.

Edward made some extraordinary changes to his character that are highly unlikely to happen in real life. At the beginning of their relationship, Edward hungered for Bella's blood. Then, when he realised he loved her profoundly, these desires disappeared. This is the reverse of the reality. If a man has aggressive urges, he is more dangerous when he loves, not less.

Another transformation in Edward was when he totally gave up his controlling habits. He became increasingly domineering with Bella during their love affair. He even imprisoned her at his house, with Alice as the jailer. Bella escaped, and Jacob whisked her away on his motorbike to La Push. After this incident, Edward realises he has been extreme in his behaviour. He admits to Bella he's been unreasonable and promises to be a reformed character. From then on he gives priority to Bella's wish for freedom.

The reality is that a controlling man is unlikely to mend his ways because the girlfriend has defied him – and gone off with a love rival that looks like Taylor Lautner.

JACOB'S TRANSFORMATION

The moment of transformation for the moody, restless Jacob was when he imprinted on Renesmee. His deep love transformed him into a gentle, tender, contented young man.

Stories are all about change, and in fiction there is no limit on the transformation that can be achieved. In fiction, the hero always turns into the man the heroine wants him to be. She doesn't love the man the way he is at the beginning of the story, but by the end he delivers what she wants. But people don't change as much as Hollywood and romantic fiction might lead you to believe.

Izzy, the real-life Bella from Chapter 10, has this to say:

'During my time with Keiran I genuinely wanted to help him change. I really thought I could. I read about how to help him with his diabetes. I made sure he ate regular meals. I reminded him about his injections.

'And I always let him know I thought him manly, even though he had an illness.

'But Keiran still wouldn't accept his illness. If I was away, he would eat junk food and mess about with his medical regime.

'As for his moods and violence, I thought I could help with those, too. I really understood him. He was like a little boy inside, hitting out because he was insecure. I thought if I poured enough love into him, it would heal him. I read books on how to help people who'd been abused as children. I thought, if he could finally be secure of my love, he would change.

'I believed he'd transform into the Keiran I wanted. I wanted him to be relaxed and confident about me going away with work. I thought he'd learn to trust through my unconditional love.

'But now when I look back on it, Keiran didn't change one little bit for all my efforts. He was still rebelling against his illness. He was still moody and jealous. He was still violent. If anything, he grew worse.'

There's a good reason Keiran didn't change. Love has great transforming power for babies and children. But not for adults. He had grown up, it was too late. There was a chance his behaviour would improve if he faced legal consequences for his actions, together with a structured psychological intervention. But transformation through love wasn't possible. If love alone cured male aggression, then there'd hardly be any. Most wives and girlfriends pour huge amounts of love and support into their men.

Izzy, understandably, didn't love Keiran the way he was. She didn't love the violent, moody, jealous man. She loved the person she thought he could be with her help. Do you love a 'bad boy' because you think he is a 'nice guy underneath? It is a good idea to ask yourself whether you really love your boyfriend as he is, the bad boy behaviour included. Or, like Izzy, are you are in love with an idea of who he could become?

ARE YOU HOPING AN INCOMPATIBLE MAN WILL CHANGE INTO A COMPATIBLE ONE?

Beth is the ambitious businesswoman from Chapter 5 who fell in love with Matt, the laid-back surfer boy who then left her for a surfer girl. This is what Beth says:

'I really loved Matt. But all through our relationship I kept waiting for him to change.

'He had his year off to "find himself" and I assumed after that he'd be different. The year would give him time to work out what he wanted to do in life and then really go for it. I suppose I thought he was like me and would commit a hundred and ten per cent to whatever he set his mind to.

'Towards the end of the year I kept ordering brochures about courses he might be interested in. And I had ideas for his own surfing school – I talked about how I could help, being in business myself. But Matt wasn't really interested. I couldn't understand it. His life was fine for a gap year, but surely he didn't want to work part-time in a surfing shop for ever, just scratching out a living?

'But that's exactly what Matt did want. I was certain he would change, grow up, get some ambitions. I was wrong.

'I was devastated when Matt finished with me and hurt he'd gone off with someone else. I was angry at everything he'd thrown away.

'We still have friends in common and I like to surf in the summer. A year after we split up I saw Matt and Layla ambling along the beach together, hand in hand. They were both in faded old clothes, carrying battered surfboards; a totally different picture to my relationship with Matt. I would drive down to the beach in my expensive work clothes, and sound the horn of my new car impatiently for him to get in so I could take him out to a nice restaurant. Everyone else must have seen we were a mismatched couple.

'I realise now I didn't really love Matt for himself. I loved the man I thought he would become. I had this image of an ambitious Matt, running his own surfing school and expanding the business through franchising. That was never the real Matt. The real man was someone happy to watch the years pass from a beloved beach, watching the seasons change but content to stay the same person.

'Good luck to him, I suppose. I'm not convinced Matt's lifestyle will make him happy in the long run, but at least he's now got a girlfriend who loves him for who he is.'

True love happens when you see your boyfriend as he is and love him anyway. If you can't accept his core nature and wish he'll change, he probably isn't your Edward or Jacob.

DOES ACCEPTING WHO HE IS MEAN THAT I HAVE TO LOWER MY EXPECTATIONS?

No. It doesn't mean you have to just put up with anything he throws at you. Dr Donald H. Baucom, a clinical psychologist, has found that people who have high standards, who want to be treated well, and expect romance and passion, are more likely to get those things. If you behave as if you value yourself highly, your boyfriend is likely to follow suit. People tend to treat you according to your own valuations of yourself, so if you behave as if you're not worth much, you are likely to get shabbier treatment, and if you ask for good treatment, you are more likely to get it. This doesn't mean a man can change his basic character, but he can treat you with decency and respect.

In *Twilight*, Edward and Jacob treat Bella as if she is wonderful and precious, even though she behaved in a way that showed she was expecting little. This works in fiction, but in reality the dynamics are that people who have low self-esteem and low standards get worse treatment.

So from the beginning, it's best to have high expectations of him. Ideas for how you can do this are spelled out in *The Rules: Time-tested Secrets for Capturing the Heart of Mr Right* by Ellen Fein and Sherrie Schneider. The principle underlying many of 'The Rules' is to behave as if you value yourself very highly and that you expect to be treated accordingly.

ARE YOU TRYING TO CHANGE YOURSELF?

Can you 'be yourself' with your boyfriend? Or are you trying to change yourself to suit him? Girls tend to be people-pleasers. But some take this too far and become human chameleons.

Just as it's important you love your man for who he is, you want him to love you the same way. Some girls don't hope their boyfriend will change. They try to change themselves instead.

Tanya, the girl in Chapter 7 who fell in love with Luke, the handsome young acting student, was an example of this:

> *'I adored Luke. I didn't want him to change at all. But I wanted to change myself.*

'*I knew I wasn't acceptable as myself to Luke and his friends, so I tried to morph into another person.*

'*I wanted to be better dressed, more refined, more literate. That way I'd be worthy of him. I spent hours trying to understand Ibsen plays. I trawled through shops trying to put together that trendy, art student look. I memorised chunks of Shakespeare, so I would have something to quote when needed. I gazed at shapeless dabs of paint at the Tate gallery of modern art and tried to understand what 'postmodern' meant. I overhauled my taste in food, or tried to. I drizzled truffle oil onto spag bol and ate oysters.*

'*At the end of our relationship, I had a mini breakdown. Someone asked me, "Tanya, what books do you like?" I couldn't answer. I had genuinely no idea. I'd forgotten what I enjoyed. I'd been ploughing through writers with Russian names for so long, I'd lost touch with what I liked. I just mumbled and looked down at my feet.*

'*Did I change, after all that effort? Not really. All that happened was I spent so long pretending to be someone else that I lost my own identity.*

'*Now I can be myself. I'm never going to try to be someone I'm not. And if someone asks me what I like reading, I can answer straight away, "I like easy reading, such as thrillers and dark romances. I can't stand anything Russian." The real me is pretty good, really, and if some man doesn't think so, then tough.*'

Bella wants to change herself in the *Twilight* story and she achieves it by the last book. She knows she can't stay as she is and have a long-term, happy relationship with Edward. But Bella had the option of becoming a vampire and completely transforming who she was. This is not an option for us in reality, and nor do you need it. Your real-life Edward or Jacob will love you for who you are now.

SECRET SIX: SUMMARY

How to know if your relationship really works:

- You have uncomplicated, great times in the beginning.
- Your personality, goals, values and lifestyles are highly compatible.
- You can accept and adjust to the differences between you.
- You are good at arguing.
- You like each other for who you are now.

The next question is, will he love you in the way you need?

CHAPTER 0

WILL HE LOVE YOU IN THE
WAY YOU NEED?

*   *   *   *
*   *

* **SECRET SEVEN** *

How to Predict
Your Future With
Your Boyfriend

(Without a crystal ball)

CHAPTER 19

WILL HE LOVE YOU IN THE WAY YOU NEED?

ARE YOU EVEN THINKING OF THE FUTURE?

Some girls go out with a man who they know isn't going to be a good boyfriend in the long run. They deliberately push away any thought of the future. They think to themselves, 'I'll just have a bit of fun' or 'At least I'm not lonely'. The problem is that if you spend time with a man, before you know it, as if by magic... you could be in love.

In *Breaking Dawn*, Bella says falling in love is like the magic in *A Midsummer Night's Dream*. If you have read Shakespeare's *A Midsummer Night's Dream*, you'll know the magic causes nothing but mischief and mayhem. In the play, Puck, a magical sprite, sprinkles a love potion on the eyes of people while they are asleep and it makes them fall in love with the first person they see when they wake. He uses it on Titania, Queen of the Fairies, and she falls in love with Bottom, a ridiculous man with an ass's head, and makes a fool of herself. *A Midsummer Night's Dream* is a comedy where everyone falls in love with the wrong people.

And in reality, love is unpredictable. Your brain is pre-programmed to fall in love, but you don't know when or with whom it will happen. Mother Nature wants you to fall in love, and like a mischievous elf, she doesn't really care if it's someone suitable or not. It's as if you did have a magical love potion sprinkled on your eyes when you were born. The potion is waiting for you to grow up and meet a man and then the magic will happen.

At the end of *A Midsummer Night's Dream* the characters are released from the spells. But there is no easy release in reality. When you fall in love you can't just fall out of love again, just because you want to. Once the spell is cast, it is very difficult to reverse.

If you spend time with a man, you might fall in love with him. Although you might tell yourself it's not serious, you cannot control the workings of your heart.

Many girls in troubled relationships say they knew it wasn't right from the start. It started off as nothing serious, just a 'casual' boyfriend. Then, before she knew it, the girl fell in love.

One trigger for love is when he falls in love with you. If you spend time with a man and he falls for you, then your mind may well respond with love for him. Research on speed dating has shown people have more positive feelings towards a date who has rated them as attractive. Adoration from a man can trigger the love potion.

Bella realises this in *Eclipse*. She can see how much Jared, one of the Quileutes, loves Kim. Kim is the classmate he has 'imprinted' on. Bella thinks about how this must feel, and how easy it would be fall in love with a person showing you this amount of devotion.

If you spend time with the wrong man, like Titania, you might fall in love with your equivalent of Bottom. The Bottom in real life won't literally have an ass's head (I hope!) but he is the man you know deep down is completely unsuited to you.

Just like in *A Midsummer Night's Dream*, in reality the wrong people fall in love all the time. Because you don't know where or when Cupid's arrow is going to strike, it's a good idea to take relationships seriously, and only spend time with men you think you might have a future with.

Or at the very least, make sure he is not Bottom.

KEEP YOUR MIND OPEN

You can't predict the future on the basis of a promising start. In the beginning of a romance, some girls see their boyfriend being incredibly kind, generous or great company and conclude these behaviours are stable traits that will carry into the future. They may be, or they may not. You can't really tell. It's best to keep an open mind. The early stages of your relationship are his 'advertising', his courtship display. He'll present himself in the best possible light in order to win your heart. He may exaggerate, fake or lie about his accomplishments and qualities.

Like adverts on TV, the product always sounds fantastic. But the reality isn't always so great when you get your hands on the actual goods.

CAN YOU PREDICT HOW HE WILL LOVE YOU?

Yes!

The key secret in this book is: *he will love you in the way his personality allows him to*. And the way he loves you is just as important as how much he loves you.

The accusation, 'You wouldn't do that if you loved me!' is often hurled between warring couples. Have you ever been confused and hurt by the fact that a boyfriend can say 'I love you' one minute, then treat you badly the next, or heard other girls complaining about this?

Your boyfriend may fall deeply in love with you, but this doesn't necessarily mean he will treat you well or love you in the way you need.

A boyfriend can only love you in the way his basic nature allows him to. So, even if he loves you deeply, if his basic nature is unkind, inconsiderate, selfish and thoughtless, then he will treat you in an unkind, inconsiderate, selfish and thoughtless way. That is his personality. He will love you in the way his personality allows him to.

For example, imagine you're in bed all day with a cold and don't receive a single text from your boyfriend asking you how you are. You may feel you're being treated badly and he doesn't care. He might love you very much, but if he's basically an inconsiderate and thoughtless kind of man, it won't occur to him to text you. You can't say, 'You wouldn't do that if you loved me!' Yes he would, because this is how an inconsiderate man loves.

Love does not transform people's basic personalities. The early heady days of romance may temporarily affect his behaviour, but if he has negative personality traits they will reappear when the excitement of new love calms down.

Girls have an idea of how love will make their boyfriends behave. But this idea may not be accurate. Our hopes about how men will behave towards us may be based on romantic fiction.

Once you have some insight into who he is you can predict how he may treat you. If you notice a stable character trait, you can predict it will be there in your future, colouring they way he behaves towards you.

When humans are transformed into vampires, they are endowed with a 'gift' that depends on their previous human personality. Bella's defining character trait was her need to look after other people. When she becomes a vampire she discovers she has a 'shield' which protects others from harm. In a similar way, your boyfriend's personality will influence the 'gift' of his love.

For example, this is the way men with the following traits are likely to love:

1) The way the agreeable man loves
If he's an agreeable, good-hearted person who generally sympathises with others, then this is how he is likely to be towards

you. His love will be expressed through kindness and sympathy. If he is not high in agreeableness – i.e. he is not interested in people, not concerned about them and doesn't feel others' emotions – then he will love you but will not pay attention to your concerns or emotions.

2) The way the man prone to negative emotions loves

If he suffers negative emotions frequently, such as anxiety, stress, sadness or anger, this will have an impact on you. As the person closest to him, you will have to deal with these difficult feelings about life. When in love with you, he will remain anxious, stressed, sad or angry around you.

3) The way the introverted man loves

If he's introverted he will love you like an introvert. He will be happy to spend time quietly with you on your own. He'll enjoy long periods of silent companionship. He will probably need some time and space away from you. If he's extroverted he will want to chat, laugh and share all his thoughts with you. His love will make him want to interact with you and others a lot and he'll want you to join him at parties.

4) The way the imaginative man loves

If he's the imaginative type he will enjoy exploring all the aspects of the experience of being in love with you. He will be verbally expressive, and he may write you love songs or poems. He is more likely to show his love in romantic ways, such as having a star named after you. Edward is imaginative in his intellectual style, so he expresses his love for Bella in beautiful words, such as his speech about life before her being like a night with no moon.

The down-to-earth type will show his love in a more conventional and practical way. He's unlikely to present you with poetry or love songs. His idea about showing his love might be to spend a day fitting wardrobes in your flat. Jacob is more down to earth and shows his feelings for Bella by helping her fix up her two motorbikes.

5) The way the conscientious man loves

A highly conscientious man will be more likely to have a strong sense of duty towards you. He'll pay attention to detail. He won't enjoy being spontaneous with you. He'll prefer you to be tidy and organised, and if you're untidy and chaotic he'll try to organise you. Edward is a highly conscientious person, so he is conscientious in the way he loves Bella. In *New Moon*, he even ends the relationship because of his strong sense of right and wrong. Jacob is less conscientious and more impulsive, so loves Bella in this style. For example, in one of his impulsive moments he tells Charlie about her having a motorbike. Edward wouldn't have done something like this, because it would have been out of character.

6) The way the contented man loves

If he's happy with life, he's likely to be satisfied with you. The dissatisfied man is likely to be restless in his relationship with you.

7) The way the unreliable man loves

If he is dishonest or unreliable generally, you can predict this will affect the way he treats you. This may seem obvious, but many girls are surprised and shocked when their boyfriend treats them badly, despite the fact that they have witnessed him treating others badly. The unreliable man will love you, but will be unreliable as a partner.

 Angela was horrified when she discovered that her boyfriend, Steve, had been cheating on her for eight

months. He had been seeing his ex-girlfriend throughout their relationship. He'd sworn it was over. Angela couldn't understand how Steve could have lied to her.

Yet when she thought about it, honesty was not one of Steve's strong points. 'I knew he regularly lied to his boss about the hours he'd worked. Once I heard him lying to his brother on the phone, saying he was ill because he didn't want to help him move house. On New Year's Eve I knew he forgot to book the taxi home, but he lied to our friends and claimed it didn't turn up – he faked a complaining phone call to the taxi firm.'

Yet Angela expected him to be honest with her. 'I knew Steve was an accomplished and convincing liar. And he showed no guilt about it. But he loved me. Surely he would treat me better, because he loved me? But the lies he told me were a hundred times worse. He played me for a fool.'

Angela's experience is typical of the way dishonest men love. Often people are more likely to be 'themselves' with their loved ones.

There are many more character traits...

No human being fits neatly into categories. In this book, I'm not able to list all the important aspects of a man's personality. Human nature is too varied. As his girlfriend, you can take time to learn about the individual characteristics of your boyfriend. You can take these into account when predicting how he'll love you.

For example, one of Edward's basic character traits is his need for control. For years he has tightly controlled his own urges, in case he gave in to his murderous impulses. His urge to control became part of his nature. When he falls in love with Bella he tries to control her. He loves her in the way his personality allows him to.

HOW CAN YOU PREDICT HOW HE WILL TREAT YOU?

By observing the patterns of his behaviour towards other people, you can work out what his negative personality traits are. No one is perfect and it is only human to show negative traits sometimes. A few negatives and one-off moments of bad behaviour are to be expected. But if you notice the same characteristic again and again, it's safe to assume this is part of his personality. Once the courtship phase is over and you've moved into a more serious stage, it's likely that he will treat you the same way you have seen him treat others.

 PSYCHOLOGY ISN'T ROCKET SCIENCE...

If he tends to put himself first with other people, he will tend to do this with you.

If he tends to 'use' other people, he will be likely to 'use' you.

If he is thoughtful to others, he will be thoughtful with you.

If he's compassionate to others, he will be compassionate to you.

If he's often critical and exacting with others, he will be with you.

If he's often dishonest to others, he will lie to you.

If he doesn't feel guilty about treating others badly, he will feel no guilt about treating you badly.

If he's angry and impatient with other people, he will be angry and impatient with you.

If you see him being unreliable with other people, he will be unreliable with you.

If he is careless of the feelings of others, he will be careless of your feelings.

If he is ungenerous with other people, he will be ungenerous to you.

Observe how he treats those with little or no power

If your man has a pattern of behaving badly to those he sees as beneath him, there's a good chance that one day he'll behave badly to you.

Examples of those with no power are animals or small children. People with little power are waiters, bar staff or others whose job it is to 'serve'. Other vulnerable types could be the elderly, or people with disabilities, or the people your boyfriend has power over at work.

If you see your man treating the weak, the defenceless or the powerless badly, then you can predict this is how he will treat you. Although the dynamics of male/female relationships often put girls in the driving seat at first, later on he will have power over you. If you fall head over heels in love with him, he'll have the power to hurt you. If you stay with him long term and have children together, you will be particularly vulnerable. One day you will need him to be kind and compassionate.

If your boyfriend generally treats the powerless with respect and kindness, it's likely he'll be the same to you.

Find out how he treated his ex

You may not like to hear this, but if your boyfriend has been in love before there is a very good chance he'll treat you in a similar way to how he treated his ex. If he treated her well, he is likely to treat you well. If he was thoughtless, cruel or selfish there's a good chance he will be like this with you.

'But I'm a different person,' you may cry, and, 'He loves me much more than he loved her.' This may be true. It won't be exactly the same. But people have stable patterns in the way they relate to others. There will be similarities in the way he treats you both.

THE FEMALE EGO (AGAIN)

Some girls like the attentions of a man who generally doesn't relate well to other human beings. They find something fascinating about the man who is always putting others down or criticising the appearance, habits or morals of others, yet who thinks his girlfriend is wonderful.

The girl takes this to mean she must be an incredibly special person, the only person worthy of his respect, the shining example amongst a bunch of unworthy mortals. There is something compelling about this, perhaps particularly for those who have low self-esteem.

Edward was a bit like this. He hardly had a good word to say about the other pupils at Forks High School and was pretty contemptuous about them on the whole. Yet he placed Bella on a pedestal. This was great for Bella's ego. She was used to being at the bottom of the pecking order among her peers, and here was the gorgeous Edward holding her high above the rest.

In the real world there are pitfalls with this.

If your boyfriend has problems relating to the rest of the human race, whether it's people in general, or girls in particular, you can safely predict these problems will end up as your problems.

You can predict that sooner or later you will begin to fall off your pedestal. You are not perfect, you have your failings and faults. Sooner or later you will disappoint him in some way and you will be in the doghouse with all the rest. 'I thought you were different,' he'll say, in a disappointed voice.

Wonderful as you are, it's unlikely a man will change his negative view of people or womankind just because of you. This happens in romantic fiction all the time, but is much rarer in real life. It's not your job as his girlfriend to prove to him that girls or mankind in general are worthwhile.

HIS KIND OF LOVING

Men and women form loving bonds with each other in different ways. There are two overall styles: secure and insecure.

These are known by psychologists as 'attachment styles'. Understanding the way your boyfriend forms close bonds with others can help you predict how he will love you.

1) The man who feels secure in relationships

The first kind of love is the 'secure' type. A man who can form secure bonds is comfortable being in a close relationship. He is happy with the feeling that others depend on him and he depends on others. He doesn't worry too much about being rejected or hurt. In *Twilight*, examples of couples with secure bonds are the vampires in the Cullen clan: Carlisle and Esme, Alice and Jasper, and Rosalie and Emmett.

2) The man who feels insecure in relationships

Relationship research has shown there are three types of 'insecure' love.

(a) Charlie Swan: the man who doesn't like to get too close

One type of insecure love is the 'dismissive' kind. This is the man who is not very comfortable with emotional intimacy. He is happy to be alone and likes to look after himself and doesn't like the idea of being dependant on anyone, or anyone depending on him. Charlie Swan is an example of this style. He is satisfied with being alone and self-sufficient. He is uncomfortable about getting involved with others. A man who loves in this way would not provide a very high level of intensity of feeling. He is only capable of giving so much. He is likely to withdraw from you emotionally if he feels too close. He doesn't think close relationships are an important part of life.

(b) Jacob Black: the man who can't get close enough

The next kind of insecurity is called the 'preoccupied' type of love. The man who has a preoccupied attachment to you wants to be very close to you. In fact, it can feel like he wants to become too close to you, almost as if he wants to get inside your head. This man often wants more than you can give. He is the clingy type, always worried that you don't love him enough. He is not happy unless he is with you. He worries about being rejected and that he's not worthy of your love. He will give a lot of intensity, which may be too much.

Jacob Black showed signs of this style of loving. Bella found he tried to get too close. He was unhappy when he was on his own. He was afraid he wasn't lovable because he was a werewolf.

Of course there is some realistic basis for Jacob's insecurities, because Bella kept rejecting him in favour of Edward. It may be that once he was in a relationship with her he would have been able to form a secure bond with her. But the way Bella experiences Jacob is what it's like to be loved by a man who is insecure in a 'preoccupied' way.

(c) Edward Cullen: the man who wants to get close, but is afraid to

The final type of insecure loving style is called the 'fearful' type. This is where the man wants to have an intimate bond with you, but is anxious about getting close. He finds it hard to trust you will be there for him. He may hide his feelings from you, because of his fear of getting hurt or losing you. He will tend to withdraw from you as a way of protecting himself. He doesn't think he is worthy of your love.

Edward showed signs of this type of insecurity. He wanted to be close to Bella but was always anxious he would lose her. He was obsessed with her safety. He hid his feelings from her. He found it very hard to believe she truly loved him. Edward finished with Bella because he wanted to 'protect' her, but it may have been as much about protecting himself. Withdrawing from her could be seen as a way of preventing the pain of rejection or loss.

DOES HE LOVE YOU IN THE WAY YOU NEED?

If your boyfriend doesn't like to get too close and has the 'dismissive' style of loving, he may not be the man for you. If you are someone who craves closeness and intensity of feeling and likes to have your boyfriend's life wrapped in your own it's likely he will never love you in the way you need.

The man with the 'clingy' or 'preoccupied' type of insecurity would not suit everyone either. You might find this type of love stifling or too 'in your face'. He might tell you he'll feel more secure when you see him every night/move in with him/get engaged, but it's as well to be cautious. His basic insecurity is unlikely to improve just because you commit.

The man who loves in a 'fearful' way can be difficult to cope with, too. This is the man who wants to be close, but is afraid to. Your boyfriend may seem close to you one minute, then withdraw from you the next. Like Bella, you may suffer great ups and downs. He doesn't trust that you will be there for him, and may find it hard to accept love from you. You may be in for an emotional see-saw ride for a very long time – perhaps forever.

DESPITE WHAT ROMANTIC FICTION LEADS YOU TO BELIEVE...

The insecure man can't really be changed by pouring love into him. The way he is capable of loving was determined years ago. His experiences of being loved as a child shaped his brain and left a permanent, or at least very long-lasting, mark.

It is no good pressurising the 'dismissive' man to get close to you. His mind is wired to give a certain amount of love... and no more. Asking him to give more is like asking a man with no legs to jump over a fence.

Similarly, asking the 'preoccupied' man to back off is like asking a starving man to stop craving food. He can't. His brain isn't made that way. He has the feeling deep inside him of 'I need more'. It can't be switched off just because it annoys you. He can mask it, or hide it, but the craving will still be there.

Finally, the 'fearful' man's anxieties can't be switched off either. If he is insecure like this, it is unlikely to be straightforward. He wants closeness, but he's uncomfortable with it. He wants intimacy, but he's scared. Imagine you are terrified of heights and someone wants you to learn to enjoy hang-gliding. You may not become truly comfortable for years – if ever.

It makes a great fictional drama when an insecure man is made secure through the power of love. But it's not true to life. In real life, the man capable of a secure attachment offers the most straightforward type of love. He'll be able to provide you with love and closeness without ambivalence or fear. He will find it easy to develop trust and show commitment.

✳ ATTACHMENT FACTS ✳

Many people fit neatly into the categories described above, and it is possible to have a different type of bond with a different person. There is a chance that people who love in an insecure way can slowly change over years, but research has shown these styles tend to be stable over time.

Psychological research has found that about a third to a half of young people are classified as 'secure' in the way they relate to others. People who can form secure bonds are more likely to report having satisfying and longer lasting relationships. A person with a secure attachment style is less likely to be depressed, anxious or lonely, and more likely to show empathy.

Secure people do not come from any particular class or educational background. And there are just as many secure women as men.

YOUR VISION OF THE FUTURE

When visualising the future, the mind plays a trick. In the same way as when you look at a distant object you can't see the detail, when you look into the future the details aren't visible. So you imagine a fuzzy picture. It doesn't have much reality in it.

And girls have a habit, when visualising the future with their man, of picturing all sorts of 'improvements'. Some girls stay with a man, not because today is great, but because they have an image of the future that looks good.

Instead of imagining a distant future, imagine you wake up tomorrow and everything between you and your boyfriend is the same as today; the only thing that has changed is that the date on the calendar has gone forward five years. Visualise your future as if it were tomorrow.

You can predict that tomorrow will be very similar to today. Tomorrow he will carry on loving you the way he does now. And you can see the fine detail of tomorrow's life together. This is what your future is likely to hold. That day in five years' time will be very similar to tomorrow in terms of his personality and your relationship.

Does it look good to you?

CHAPTER 20

IS HE YOUR EDWARD?
IS HE YOUR JACOB?

HOW YOU FEEL ABOUT HIM

Your feelings will tell you whether your boyfriend could be your true love or not. You need to listen to your heart.

But feelings are not the only things to take into account. Just because you have strong feelings for a man, it doesn't mean he's the right one for you. You can be strongly attracted to a person who won't make you happy. Loving something doesn't mean they are good for you. The overweight person loves food. The problem gambler loves gambling.

As well as your emotions, you have eyes and a brain. To find your true love you need to harness your powers of perception and judgment.

But what is true love and how do you know when you've found it?

LOVING HIM AS HE REALLY IS

True love is based on knowing the truth about each other. It's knowing each other deep down and still loving what you see. It is love which is firmly grounded in reality, not illusion. Rosalie didn't find true love with Royce King the Second because her feelings were based on a false image of who he was.

In one of the books Stephenie Meyer has enjoyed, *Gone with the Wind*, there is another good example of love based on illusion. Scarlett O'Hara spends almost all her time in love with a man called Ashley, not Rhett Butler. At the very end of the book Scarlett realises she doesn't truly love Ashley after all. Instead, she was in love with a fantasy of who he was. She had an image in her mind of who her true love would be and she had superimposed this fantasy onto Ashley. She says, 'I loved something I made up.' The Ashley she loved never existed at all, except in her imagination.

As a *Twilight* fan your fantasy image is probably like Edward or Jacob. Like Scarlett and Rosalie, you need to ask yourself honestly whether you love your man as he really is.

LOVING HIM AS HE IS NOW

True love is where you love your man for who he is today, not for who you hope he'll become tomorrow.

We can't change anything we like. We are led to believe these days that our man can grow and change if we 'work' at the relationship. But time and again, psychology research reveals that people have stable character traits. When you are in love with a man but keep hoping he'll undergo a radical change, it is not true love. He (and you) may mature in some ways, but this is not inevitable and may take years. If you need him to transform his character, then you don't truly love him.

HE IS CAPABLE OF BEING 'TRUE' TO YOU

True love also means he will be 'true', in the sense that he'll be faithful and loyal to you. Some men aren't built this way. You can't have true love with a man who has a habit of being disloyal or unfaithful. A good boyfriend will be like Edward and Jacob, in that he will be comfortable with the idea of monogamy and capable of showing loyalty.

The Truth About Love

True love is based on a true understanding about the nature of love. Some people have an idealised or unrealistic vision of love. There are three key ways that real true love is different from true love in fiction:

1) Love is not unbreakable

If it were, there would be few break-ups, few divorces. True love is breakable. But this doesn't detract from its value. Some of the most valuable things in life are fragile and are no less precious for it. In fact, they may be more precious. For example, think of an antique crystal vase, a Fabergé egg, a famous painting, an ancient silk tapestry. Despite being fragile, they endure, because they are looked after and treated as valuable.

Similarly, if you realise love is breakable, you will value it and look after it better, so it is more likely to last forever.

Love flourishes under certain conditions and dies in others. It can't survive everything.

2) Love is not a matter of life and death

For a child, love is a matter of life and death. An unloved child may die. A parent will die for their children.

But as an adult you can live happily without romantic love. You can lose love and your heart will heal and you can love again.

3) Love is not unconditional

True love can be long-lasting and strong but it is not like the love of a mother for a child. Love is an equal exchange between grown-ups, where you both give and get something back.

You are no longer a child and you do not need unconditional love from a boyfriend. As an adult, you have adult obligations to your boyfriend, and he to you. This means there are some conditions attached to your love. If he shows, after a prolonged period of time, that he is not capable of meeting your needs as a woman, your love may die. And the same applies to him.

HAVE YOU FOUND THE LOVE OF YOUR LIFE?

This book has been an exploration of who you are, what you want and what sort of real-life man can make you happy. Here are ten crucial questions to ask when judging whether a man is your true love:

1) Is he capable of – and interested in – fulfilling your needs on a more serious basis?

Some relationships work well if you only see each other once a week for fun and good times. But this doesn't mean you can fulfil each other at a deeper level. Some men might make a great casual boyfriend. But if you shared your lives on a more intimate level, such as living together, could you see it working? If the answer is 'probably not', he is not your Edward or Jacob.

2) Is he similar to you?

Your true love will be compatible with you in the areas of personality, goals and lifestyle that are important to you. Opposites can attract but are less likely to last long term.

3) Can you live with his differences?

True love involves compromise, tolerance and accepting him as he is today. Rather than hoping he'll change to suit you, you'll find ways of living happily with his differences.

4) Can you live with his good points?

You might realise that it's a good idea to take account of his flaws and faults. But just as important, can you live with his great qualities?

Many girls are very attracted to certain aspects of their man, only to find these qualities are the very things that turn them off when the relationship goes sour. For example, you might love the fact your boyfriend treats his mother well. You see this as part of his kind and loving nature. But will you love going to his mother's every Sunday for lunch because he doesn't want to disappoint her? Or you might love your boyfriend's sensitivity, then discover it has a downside. He's over-sensitive at times. He sulks if you say the 'wrong' thing or if he sees a 'put-down' in your innocent remark.

Most of a man's good points will have their pitfalls, and many girls don't see them coming. So when you think of the future, predict that his good points will have a down side. Can you live with them?

5) Is he your best friend?

Couples in long-term, happy relationships often describe their partner as their 'best friend'. The physical attraction is there too, but underneath this they really like their partner as a person and enjoy their company. However, some couples love each other, but don't like each other. They wish they could switch off their romantic feelings, because deep down they don't respect their partner.

From his research on relationships, John Gottman has discovered 70 per cent of the satisfaction reported by couples depends on the quality of the friendship they share. This is true for both men and women.

It may not feel natural to see a boyfriend as a friend, particularly if you are young. It's likely that, for much of your childhood, boys either ignored you or jeered at you. Childhood friendships between boys and girls are not very common. Young boys and young girls generally don't get on. This all changes in adolescence. But you may not be used to being friends with a male and have low expectations about how he will treat you.

Your true love will be a male best friend who you find physically attractive. You know he's not your Edward or Jacob if you don't like who he is, or if he's not being a good friend to you.

6) How good are your good times – and how many are there?
If you have far more good times together than bad, then you are likely to stay together.

7) Can you argue well?
Do you and he make 'repair attempts' when arguing? If you manage to avoid the Four Horsemen: criticism, contempt, defensiveness and stonewalling, then you can predict you may have a good future.

8) Can he share the decision-making with you?
John Gottman has discovered that relationships where the man refuses to share the decision-making are relationships which don't last.

He found there was an 81 per cent chance of divorce in marriages where the husband has a habit of failing to take his wife's views into account. What's needed is what Gottman calls 'accepting influence' – your partner accepts your input in decisions. Gottman believes it is essential for happy relationships.

He has found almost all women naturally think about their man's feelings when making a decision. But a significant number of men don't do this for their wife or girlfriend.

You can predict that if, despite your best efforts, your boyfriend habitually fails to take your views and feelings into account, your relationship is likely to end.

Or looking at it positively, if your boyfriend normally respects and considers your feelings as part of his decision-making process, this is a very good sign for your future.

9) Is he a 'bad boy'?

You can't have true love with a 'bad boy'.

The bad boy is the man who is domineering, dangerous and aggressive. Women fall in love with men like this all the time.

These bad boys are known as 'boys' because they haven't properly grown up into men. Like the 'immortal children', the child vampires in *Breaking Dawn*, they are stuck in their emotional development. The immortal children have temper tantrums which cause immense destruction. The bad boy can't control his anger and has temper tantrums like a child. And bad boys take what they want, with no consideration of others. They are needy and greedy, like spoilt toddlers.

Bella dreams that one of the immortal children kills everyone she loves. Having an 'immortal child' in your life will bring you destruction and pain.

But the child-like nature of the bad boy is attractive to many. He can be very charming. Like the child vampires in *Twilight*, he causes strong emotional reactions in others. Women can't help loving him. The bad boy appeals to the nurturing, motherly part of a woman.

And once a woman's nurturing instinct is switched on, it is difficult to switch off. Motherly love is strong.

Romantic fiction leads you to believe you can transform the immortal child or bad boy into somebody gentler and calmer. But you can't. Like the immortal children, the bad boy can't be tamed.

Another kind of bad boy, at the less extreme end, is the restless risk taker, the man with a 'wandering eye', or a difficult personality. He is not likely to provide true love either. This kind of bad boy, although appealing in the short term, is unlikely to provide the lasting love and loyalty you want from a boyfriend.

Romantic fiction, like *Twilight*, might tempt you to believe you can have a bad boy who is also a nice guy. In reality you can't have both. You can't have a bad boy who is really a nice guy underneath, no matter what the love songs and stories tell you.

10) Is he a 'nice guy'?

Your true love is more likely to be a nice guy. He has a good ability to get on with people, is kind, thoughtful and willing to invest in a long-term, monogamous relationship.

This does not mean he is overly submissive, weak and unable to command respect from others. He will be his own person and have inner strength. Women do not like men to be 'too' nice, where niceness crosses over into to being far too eager to please. This is the Mike Newton 'wagging tail' syndrome. This type of man is not attractive to women, as he is too easy to dominate. Most women don't want a man they can boss around, they want an equal.

A GOOD MAN

So the happy medium may be to look for a 'good man' to be your true love. This is a man who is confident in himself while being willing take your thoughts and feelings into account. The lucky in love recognise a good man when they see one. The unlucky in love don't. This is nothing to do with lack of intelligence, or lack of ability. Girls who are unlucky in love often have great powers of judgement when it comes to other areas of their lives.

For example, some girls will put huge efforts into planning their perfect wedding. They try on dress after dress. They send it back because the beading was the wrong shape. They reflect for hours about the right venue, spend hours pouring over swathes of fabric, choose just the right shade to complement their skin, ponder for hours who should sit with whom. They have a fantastic wedding.

If only they had put as much thought into their choice of groom.

SECRET SEVEN: SUMMARY

How to predict the future with your boyfriend:

- Only date a man with whom you may have a future.
- He will love you according to his personality.
- He will treat you the way he treats others.
- Assume he will carry on being himself.
- Understand his attachment style.
- Understand the reality of true love.
- Recognise the signs of a long-lasting relationship.

CHAPTER 21

WHY YOUR RELATIONSHIP DECISIONS – AND *TWILIGHT* – ARE IMPORTANT

WHY YOUR ROMANTIC PARTNER CHOICE IS VITAL – AND NOT JUST TO YOU

A girl's choice of boyfriend does not just matter to them. It is important to the human race. One day you will choose a man who'll be the father of your children. His traits will be handed down to the next generation. You will play your part in shaping humanity.

In the animal kingdom, female partner choice has shaped whole species. The peacock has developed its tail because the peahens like it. The more beautiful his tail, the more girlfriends the peacock gets. His sons have lovely tails like dad. The son with the best tail gets the most girls. And so on. One of the most beautiful sights in nature, the peacock's tail, exists because females chose it.

The power of female choice applies to humans, too. Throughout most of prehistory, men and women lived together in hunter-gatherer groups and women were relatively free to choose their mate. Girls preferred men with 'manly looks' such as square jaws, slim hips and wide shoulders. This is why gorgeous men like Taylor Lautner and Robert Pattinson exist.

If by some genetic chance a man was born with diamond skin like Edward's, you can bet the girls would queue up to go out with him. He would have plenty of sparkly boy babies, who would have plenty of girlfriends when they grew up. In time, boys without diamond skin might die out, because they couldn't get a wife.

You can imagine two girls talking together in the future about one of these unfortunate men: 'And do you know, there we were in full sunlight, and his skin didn't even gleam. I didn't know where to look, I was so disgusted. And he had the cheek to ask me out. I thought, "As if," and walked away.'

But the power of female choice to shape the human race is not just about looks. In his book *The Mating Mind*, psychologist Geoffrey Miller says that female partner choice explains why humans have big brains. The clever men impressed the girls. And traits such as kindness, faithfulness, compassion and generosity can be passed down the generations, too.

Romantic partner choice is not a trivial matter, regardless of how much some older people and men tend to scorn a girl's preoccupation with boys.

Nowadays we have more freedom and choice about boyfriends than ever before. Once again, females have the power to shape the next generation.

You owe it to yourself and your descendants to pick a good one. The future of the human race is in your hands!

A DIFFICULT CHOICE

Women have the freedom to choose their boyfriends again today but we live in a different world to our hunter-gatherer ancestors. There are far more men to select from, you will live longer and have higher expectations. So decision-making regarding boyfriends is far more complex.

But Mother Nature, like the mischievous Puck in *A Midsummer Night's Dream*, doesn't care about your long-term personal fulfilment. She wants you to bond with someone who will give you babies. Mother Nature did not equip you to choose for long-term happiness. In fact, it used to be important that you weren't too fussy as there were fewer men around.

Nowadays, you need to be very discriminating about who you fall in love with – if you want long-term happiness. But instead of helping you make better choices, some aspects of modern life steer you to bad ones. The amount of romantic fiction, films, and love songs we are exposed to is huge. We even study them in school. In *New Moon*, Bella complains about having to study romances when she is broken-hearted.

To repeat the message throughout this book: romantic fiction does not encourage good judgment. It contains unrealistic messages about love and relationships. It provides fantasy figures for you to fall in love with and superimpose on real men, as Rosalie does with the brutal Royce King the Second, when she imagines him to be a Prince Charming figure. Romantic fiction encourages you to believe you can happily bond with an incompatible man. It encourages you to believe you can have a blissful love life with a difficult or even dangerous man.

Girls pick the wrong man all the time, particularly when they are new to the world of relationships. Bella was 18 when she married Edward and was quite rightly nervous of this. In the US, 40 per cent of couples who marry under the age of 20 are divorced ten years later. In reality, teen marriages are likely to be short-lived. At this age most people are not ready to make a good choice of life partner for themselves.

Sadly, some girls are never ready. They make the same relationship mistakes over and over again, or make different mistakes each time. They get embroiled in a bad relationship that leaves them damaged, so damaged they end up even less capable of choosing good man. A lot of unnecessary unhappiness is caused by poor romantic partner choice.

GIRL POWER

In fact, many people believe that young girls having the power to make good relationship choices for themselves is the key to eliminating not only suffering, but to eliminating poverty and changing the world. People have begun to realise that the dilemmas of teenage girls are important.

If a young girl in the Third World is educated, looked after, and able to earn her own money she will make choices which will not only make her life better, but make the world better. When she has the power to make the best romantic choices for herself, she will marry later and have fewer children. She will invest 90 per cent of her income in her family, a far higher proportion than men do. Her children will grow up, happy, healthy and educated, with the power to make good choices for themselves.

There is good evidence that investing in young girls is the best way to fight global poverty, death in childbirth and AIDS. Yet only a tiny fraction of foreign aid goes to girls.

You can watch a video about why the girl is a powerful force for change on thegirleffect.org.

Female romantic partner choice, far from being a trivial topic, has a profound significance for the rest of the world.

WHY THE *TWILIGHT* SERIES IS IMPORTANT

Some people look down on *Twilight*. You may have been annoyed by people who've sneered at the books or movies, without ever having read or seen them. It's something all fans put up with.

The *Twilight* series is far more than just an enjoyable story about a young girl, a vampire and a werewolf. It is significant because it captures the 'spirit of our times'. The books deal with our deepest hopes and fears: the longing for love, acceptance, sex, belonging, family, perfection, beauty, power and the fear of ageing and death. *Twilight* shows us how we feel about these eternal dilemmas at this point in our history. It is full of insights into human nature and relationships. *Twilight* deals with the longings of the twenty-first-century young woman. The longings of young women, so long ignored or belittled in history, are now a major force in shaping the world.

When you talk about the characters and stories in *Twilight*, you are talking about topics which all great thinkers and writers have grappled with for centuries. *Twilight* is as important – in its own way – as Shakespeare.

WHEN PEOPLE 'DISS' *TWILIGHT*

Plenty of people dismiss young women's concerns as trivial, and are scornful of *Twilight*. If anyone scorns it you can say (and it may help to say it in a cold, superior tone of voice), 'Yes, *Twilight* can appear trivial to the superficial eye. But when you look at it more deeply you realise that the story encapsulates the existential dilemmas that are an integral part of the human condition. Meyer cleverly uses literary allusion, drawing from Shakespeare, Brontë and Austen and the Gothic tradition to do this. I think *Twilight* successfully captures the zeitgeist of the twenty-first century, this very pivotal point in human evolution – what's your analysis?'

FINALLY

There are important relationship lessons and insights hidden in *Twilight*. Behind the fantasy of vampires and werewolves lie secrets that all girls should know.

Finding your true love is having the ability to realise when a man is not your Edward or Jacob, and the ability to spot the man who is.

Girls who are 'lucky' in love are able to do this. Is it luck? No, it is skill – a skill they may not be aware they have, but a skill nonetheless. They can harness their powers of perception and judgment when it comes to men. Like everyone who is good at making complex decisions, they often have difficulty explaining how they do it. Their success is a secret, even to themselves. They just say 'it feels right'. Their intuition and feelings guide them to the right decision.

The secrets are there in *Twilight*, lying beneath the exciting fictional story. You too can be lucky in love if you follow the steps:

Secret One: deepen your understanding of the nature of love and attraction by understanding how *Twilight* appeals to the innermost workings of your heart.

Secret Two: learn to recognise the pitfalls of romantic wishful thinking so you can spot the man who can't make you happy.

Secret Three: move away from the fantasy Edward and Jacob, and instead develop positive expectations about real-life men.

Secret Four: develop your self-awareness. Knowing yourself better will help you know what you need and don't need from a man. Recognise when your personal baggage is interfering with your relationship choices.

Secret Five: improve your powers of judgment of men. Recognise the common pitfalls when judging men.

Secret Six: recognise when your relationship is working and not working.

Secret Seven: make accurate, insightful predictions about your future together.

TRUE LOVE EXISTS

Despite all its pitfalls, love is a wonderful thing and is worth finding.

Not everybody is lucky enough to find a man with whom they can have the exciting 'in love' feeling last for decades, but many of us can expect to find years of contentment with a loving partner. You can find love whatever your looks, whoever you are. Good looks have nothing to do with finding true love. If it did, Hollywood romances would be the most long-lasting in the world.

The secret of true love is to find the right man. The secret to finding the right man is to know who you are and what sort of man you need. The secret of a happy relationship is to understand real love, not the romantic fantasy.

I would wish you luck. But it's not just a question of luck; it's about using your powers of perception and judgment. When you use them you have a good chance of finding happiness and fulfilment with your real-life Edward or Jacob.

FURTHER READING

Baron-Cohen, Simon *The Essential Difference* (2003, Allen Lane).

Eckman, Paul *Emotions Revealed: Understanding Faces and Feelings* (2003, Weidenfeld & Nicolson).

Fein, Ellen & Schneider, Sherrie *The Rules: Time-tested Secrets for Capturing the Heart of Mr Right* (1995, Warner Books).

Gottman, John & Silver, Nan *The Seven Principles for Making Marriage Work* (1999, Crown Publishers).

Wiseman, Richard *The Luck Factor: Change Your Luck – and Change Your Life* (2003, Century).

WHERE TO GO FOR HELP

In the *Twilight* story, Bella's unhappiness, loneliness and low self-esteem were cured by the love of a dangerous man. In reality, personal problems can't be solved like this.

If you have personal difficulties, please confide in someone you trust among your own family or friends. If there is no one you can talk to, or your family and friends can't help you then here are some organisations that could help:

- Your local GP practice. Your doctor can refer you to a counsellor, psychologist or other appropriate specialist.

- Your school, college or university. Most of them provide a confidential counselling/welfare service for students.

- Your workplace. If you work for a large organisation, they may have a personal support service for employees.

- Local voluntary organisations. There are many different organisations that provide help for people living in particular locations. Do a Google search with the name of your area and the type of difficulty you have or the type of help you are looking for.

- National organisations. Here are details of just some of the UK-wide organisations which may be able to either help you directly or give you information about where to find help:

- BullyingUK: Offers online support by email for young people worried about bullying.
  Website: www.bullying.co.uk

- ChildLine: Confidential helpline for children and young adults experiencing problems. Telephone: 0800 1111 (Free 24-hour helpline)
  Website: www.childline.org.uk

- Get Connected: Helpline, emails and web chat for the under-25s struggling with any problem. Telephone: 0808 808 4994 (Calls free, open 1–11 p.m. every day)
  Website: www.getconnected.org.uk

- MIND: Information and advice line for people of all ages experiencing mental distress. Calls from landlines are charged at local rates, mobile phone charges vary. Telephone: 0845 766 0163 (open Monday to Friday, 9–5 p.m.)
  Website: www.mind.org.uk

- Refuge: Helpline and advice for women, young people and children worried about domestic violence.
  Telephone: 0808 2000 247 (Free 24-hour helpline)
  Website: www.refuge.org.uk

- Samaritans: Emotional support helpline to all those experiencing despair, distress or suicidal feelings. Calls from landlines are 2p per minute, plus 7p call set-up fee, mobile phone charges vary.
  Telephone: 08457 90 90 90 (UK and N. Ireland) 1850 60 90 90 (Ireland) (24-hour helplines)
  Website: www.samaritans.org

By buying this book you've helped young girls who have no realistic hope of enjoying a happy romantic life.

Many girls today are forced into marriage whilst still a child or young teenager, often with an older man chosen for her by someone else. A high proportion of these girls will die in childbirth because pregnancy is risky for young girls with immature bodies.

Twenty per cent of net author royalties from the sale of this book will go to a project called Berhane Hewan, which promotes education for girls in Ethiopia. It helps to prevent them from becoming child brides by providing an incentive – a sheep worth $25 – to families who keep their girls in school.

This project is just one of many supported by The Girl Effect, a campaign to improve the lives of young girls in poor countries. A girl who is cared for, educated and given choices will have fewer pregnancies and greater earning power, so that she can look after and educate her own children. This stops the cycle of poverty from affecting the next generation. This is the Girl Effect.

To find out more about why girls are a powerful force for change, watch this video: **http://www.girleffect.org/question**

To find out more about the project supported by this book go to: **http://www.globalgiving.org/projects/berhane-hewan-reducing-child-marriage-in-ethiopia**